THE POWER OF
YOUR OTHER HAND

OTHER BOOKS BY LUCIA CAPACCHIONE

The Creative Journal: The Art of Finding Yourself
The Creative Journal: A Guide for Parents, Teachers and Counselors of Children and Adolescents
The Creative Journal: A Handbook for Teens
The Well-Being Journal: The Art of Self-Care
Co-authored with Elizabeth Johnson, *The Lighten Up Journal: Making Friends with Your Body*
Audio Tape: *Well-Being Journal Meditations*

For information regarding LUCIA CAPACCHIONE's books, lectures, workshops, and consultations contact:

INNERWORKS
1341 Ocean Avenue #100
Santa Monica, CA 90401
(213) 285-9489

THE POWER OF YOUR OTHER HAND

A course in channeling the inner wisdom of the right brain.

LUCIA CAPACCHIONE

NEWCASTLE PUBLISHING CO., INC.
NORTH HOLLYWOOD, CALIFORNIA
1988

ISBN 0-87877-130-1

Edited by Hank Stine and Janrae Frank
Cover/Book Design by Riley K. Smith

The author of this book does not dispense medical advice nor prescribe the use of any technique as a form of treatment for medical problems without the advice of a physician, either directly or indirectly. The intent of the author is only to offer information of a general nature to help you cooperate with your doctor in your mutual quest for health. In the event you use any of the information in this book for yourself, you are prescribing for yourself, which is your constitutional right, but the author and publisher assume no responsibility for your actions.

For permissions, see p. viii.

A NEWCASTLE BOOK
First printing, April 1988
10 9 8 7 6 5 4 3 2
Printed in the United States of America

Dedicated
with
love and gratitude
to
my teachers:

GURUMAYI CHIDVILASANANDA
Meditation Master

TOBE REISEL
Art Therapist

CORITA KENT
Artist
(1918–1986)

THANKS

to the contributors:
Mona Brookes
Molly Deane Clarke
Dorothy Gilles
Tom D. Gumas, M.D.
Elizabeth Johnson
Pamela Karle
Erin King-West
Kadi Kurgpold
Sylvia Miller
Jeanne Paige
Aleta Pearce
Brad Stoller

to all the students and clients
who helped field test the material in this book

to all those who gave encouragement along the way

to my daughter, Aleta Pearce
and my friends, Nancy Shaw & Jim Strohecker
for their love and invaluable support
while assisting with research, typing, word processing, editing,
and doing lots of hand-holding with me while this book was being born

to the editors, Hank Stine and Janrae Frank
for their knowledgeable guidance and great enthusiasm,
for encouraging me to stretch
and enrich this book and my own understanding

to the designer, Riley Smith
for his sensitivity, skill, depth of understanding,
and for leading me to the book's publisher

to my publisher, Al Saunders
for providing the best support an author could receive
and for being a fine human being

Table of Contents

Grateful acknowledgement is made to the following for permission to reprint copyrighted material:

Ohio University Press: Quotations from *The Creative Journal: The Art of Finding Yourself*, by Lucia Capacchione. Copyright © 1980 by Ohio University Press.

SYDA Foundation: A portion of "Breakthrough into Insight," by Joseph Chilton Pearce, from *Darshan* No. 2 (1987). Copyright © 1987 by SYDA Foundation. All rights reserved.

Jeremy P. Tarcher, Inc. : Excerpts from *Drawing on the Right Side of the Brain*, by Betty Edwards. Copyright © 1979 by Betty Edwards.

Jeremy P. Tarcher, Inc.: Excerpts from *Joy's Way*, by W. Brugh Joy, M.D. Copyright © 1979 by W. Brugh Joy, M.D.

Lothrop, Lee & Shepard Co.: A portion of *Handedness: Right and Left*, by Ira S. Wile. Copyright © 1934 by Lothrop, Lee & Shepard, a division of William Morrow & Co.

Harper & Row and Literistic Ltd.: Excerpts from *Love, Medicine & Miracles*, by Bernie S. Siegel, M.D. Copyright © 1986 by B. H. Siegel, S. Korman, and A. Schiff, Trustees of the Bernard S. Siegel, M.D., Children's Trust. Reprinted by permission of Harper & Row Publishers and the author's agent.

Dell Publishing Co., Inc.: A portion of *Mind as Healer, Mind as Slayer*, by Kenneth R. Pelletier. Copyright © 1977 by Dell Publishing Co., Inc.

Shambhala Publications, Inc.: Excerpts from *On the Way to the Wedding*, by Linda Schierse Leonard. Reprinted by arrangement with and copyright © 1986 by Shambhala Publications, Inc.

Viking Penguin, Inc., New York: A portion of *The Psychology of Consciousness*, by Robert E. Ornstein. Copyright © 1972, 1977, 1986 by Robert E. Ornstein. Reprinted by permission of Viking Penguin, Inc.

University of Chicago Press: Portions of *Right and Left: Essays on Dual Classification*, edited by Rodney Needham. Copyright © 1973 by University of Chicago Press. Table ("Scheme of Meru Symbolic Classification") reprinted from *Africa* 30 (1960): 20–33, International African Institute, London. Table 1 from "Symbolic Values and the Integration of Society Among the Mapuche of Chile," reprinted from *American Anthropologist* 64 (1962): 6, American Anthropological Association, Washington, D.C. Not for further reproduction.

SYDA Foundation: Excerpt from *Understanding Siddha Yoga*, by Swami Muktananda. Copyright © 1978 by SYDA Foundation. All rights reserved.

Harrison House: Quotations from *Chagall by Chagall*, by Marc Chagall. Copyright © 1982 by Harrison House.

Foreword

As I traveled through life helping teachers and their students to draw, the name Lucia Capacchione surfaced over and over. I was told that I must meet her because we were doing the same work in different form. I was assured that she too could pull out hidden abilities that are so often buried inside of us. I was told that she created magic with children and helped them express themselves through writing in journals. Our first meeting spilled over with excitement. We shared our experiences and our visions. We talked about a future generation of children who were not blocked from their inner feelings and enjoyed productive ways of expressing themselves.

After our meeting had run long over the time alloted, we concluded that we wanted to do a project that would allow us to work together. We felt that one of the best ways we could integrate each other's work was to experience it ourselves. Lucia came to my drawing classes and I proceeded to do her Journal work. I will be forever grateful for the process I experienced through her work, as well as the wonderful successes we have shared in our collaborations.

Lucia has included some of my otherhanded writings and drawings in this book. They accurately represent the kind of breakthroughs I made using her techniques. In one of the first exercises I was struggling with the mundane problems of teacher turnover in my Monart Drawing School. The solution was evading me and my mind felt exhausted. During a meditation I asked for guidance and a path that would help me deal with this problem. To my surprise my left hand spelled out an answer. It said, "Don't ever forget the children. Relate! Love!"

Up to that point I had been following all the regular business advice on how to deal with employees, none of which was really changing the conditions or helping me with my frustration. This unexpected answer washed over me like a cosmic truth. The children were what it was all about. Even though I continued facing problems in running a business, my reaction was completely changed. Now, when the administrative part of my work overwhelms me I go to my drawing school. I sit and draw with the children, relate to them and love them. This never fails to make me feel it is all worth it.

Receiving such guidance from my own left hand was a transforming experience. I actually felt as if someone else was talking to me and giving me advice that I could trust. It had the ring of reliable truth. I felt this happen again and again as I used my left hand to explore my thoughts and feelings.

On another occasion I had an unforgettable breakthrough. It dawned on me that if I analyzed how my dominant hand functioned I could reverse the process for the other hand. That seems like a simple deduction, yet it took me several days to come to it. At that point the quality of writing with my left hand came under my control. The importance of such a discovery was that it taught me a basic principle that I could apply to other areas of my life. I learned that if I take the time and patience to understand a particular function I can apply that understanding to similar functions.

As for drawing with the other hand, what fun! Even for someone as confident about drawing as myself, it was amazing to me how well I was able to draw with my left hand. If I hadn't met Lucia, I might never have tried such a thing or imagined the ramifications. In my personal life I had been struggling with healing myself of physical illness through movement and meditation practices. After I started using my left hand I realized that a truly well body is a whole body. I began doing exercises where I used the left side of my body with equal agility and grace as my right. These practices were definitely a part of the wellness that has now blessed me for years.

It is not really surprising that these ambidexterous exercises ultimately enabled me to do something I never dreamed I could do: DANCE. Shyness had always prevented me from even attempting dance, even though I had a secret longing. Who would have guessed that along with all the other transformational work I was doing I would develop enough self-confidence to dance for the first time? Within five years dance had become a central part of my life. I never anticipated that I would perform before live audiences or dance in a video.

These personal experiences enable me to recommend Lucia's work wholeheartedly. If you explore the material presented in this book and let it lead you into yourself, you too may be amazed at the results.

I meet many artists and educators who are on the leading edge of changing things through "possibility thinking." They weave with a common thread. It always seems to involve breaking old patterns and seeing things with a new perspective. Using your non-dominant hand and learning its lessons is one of the most powerful tools you can use toward that goal.

MONA BROOKS
Educator and Author of
Drawing with Children:
A Method that Works for Adults, Too

Author's Introduction

I'd always considered myself a right-handed person. Like most people, I believed I couldn't write with the *other hand.* I tried it once, when I was about ten or eleven, and found that my left hand preferred to write in mirror fashion from right to left.

That's curious, I thought, and promptly dismissed my left hand for being so "backward." Over the years, I gave it other auxiliary tasks to perform. It played a supporting role on the piano, held the paper while I wrote stories or drew pictures, and so on.

I didn't write again with my left hand until twenty years later. I was struggling with a life-threatening illness which, I learned later, was a collagen disease. Collagen is the connective tissue in the body; the glue, so to speak. I had literally "come unglued."

At the medical clinic I was run through a series of tests and given various medications in what appeared to be a hit-or-miss fashion. A lab test mix-up, false diagnosis, incorrect prescription and medication led to many side effects. For weeks I struggled with this debilitating illness which baffled the doctors and terrified me.

In desperation over the ineffectual attempts of a string of medical specialists to "cure" me, I turned inward. I began keeping a personal journal of my feelings and thoughts about the illness, the doctors, my life, and myself. I stopped taking medication and started concentrating on journal-keeping. It was the only thing that gave me relief. It also helped me develop enough insight and courage to enter psychotherapy for the first time.

My therapist, a young woman named Bond, used an eclectic blend of Transactional Analysis, Gestalt Therapy, and Neo-Reichian breathing and body exercises. Using dramatic role-play techniques from Gestalt Therapy, she had me move around the room and "act out" the different parts of my personality. She introduced me to concepts and terms from Transactional Analysis: The Inner Parent, the Inner Child, and the Adult. She explained that they all lived side by side within me.

The Inner Parent consisted of inner voices that could be critical or nurturing. In order to help me face the Critical Parent and render it less powerful, Bond directed me to "act it out." I actually became that character who chattered away in my head, nagging at my self-esteem and sabotaging me. Adopting up-tight body language and a cranky tone of voice, I said things like: "You'll never amount to anything" or "You're lazy. Get to work" or "Look how stupid you are. You made a mistake. When will you ever learn?" Bond also let me give voice to the Nurturing Parent, the part of me that is tender and compassionate. And she helped me turn this mothering ability inward upon myself. I'll never forget the therapy session in which I cradled an imaginary baby in my arms and realized the baby was me: my Inner Child. As I did this, I remembered a picture I had drawn during the most difficult days of my illness. I had named it, "Giving Birth to Myself."

Bond also encouraged me to reach down deep into old feelings that I had squashed in childhood. She helped me understand that feelings come from my little Inner Child, who was still alive in me although very wounded. She had been forced to numb certain feelings early on because I got punished or ridiculed for expressing them. Feelings like anger, sadness, fear were considered bad. If I had "bad" feelings I was made to feel like a "bad" person. My Inner Child first appeared as a feisty little kid. She was in a rage, yelling and screaming at the doctors who had been so cold, uncaring, and inept. I found myself stomping all over the room like a two-year-old. I pretended the doctors were in an

August 13. 1973

overstuffed chair Bond had in her office, and I beat them up with a tennis racquet. What a relief!

At the close of our second session, Bond sat me down on the floor. She smiled secretively and placed a huge pad of newsprint in front of me. Thrusting a big, fat kindergarten crayon into my *left* hand, she instructed me.

"I want you to write a contract with yourself," she instructed. "Write down what you're going to do this week to apply what you've learned in this session." Noticing my puzzled expression, she went on, "Yes, I know you're right-handed. I *want* you to use your left hand for this." So I printed in slow, deliberate strokes. Big, awkward yet bold letters declared:

GIVE MYSELF
PERMISSION
TO LET MY CHILD OUT
AND FEEL MY
FEELINGS AND
SAY I'M O.K.!!

As my untutored hand haltingly struggled to form the words, I felt myself regress to about four years old, the age I was when my father taught me to print my own name. Bond later remarked that my appearance changed as I wrote. My face became the face of a very young child, with lips pursed and brow furrowed in deep concentration as I labored over this difficult task. Through body language and voice—as I spoke the words I was writing—I became that little girl. I actually shifted into my favorite floor-sitting position from childhood, with knees bent, touching each other, and feet out on both sides.

Afterward, I felt light and giggly, as if a giant weight had been lifted from my shoulders. It seemed like magic and it was so simple. After that I started expressing feelings more in my everyday life, telling people what I wanted and what I didn't want. Then my Playful Child came out and I started having more fun. The more my Little Child came out, the more I liked her, even when she was mad. I started feeling much better physically. My creative energy was recharged as well, and the Adult part of me (who makes decisions and plans) was able to go back to work on a new design project. But this time, my Adult took my Creative Child to work with her so that the new design project was fun. I had embraced that child-like part of me: the heart of my creativity and aliveness. At long last, I was integrating her into the rest of my life. *I had come home to myself.*

I continued writing and drawing in my journal where I discovered I could carry on the Gestalt-type conversations with my Inner Parent and Inner Child. Only now the dialogues were written with my right hand and left hand. My dominant right hand wrote the Inner Parent voices. My Inner Child spoke through my left hand. In the terminology of Gestalt Therapy my right hand expressed the "top dog" (the controlling, overbearing Critical Parent part of me). My left hand reflected the feelings of the "underdog" (the part that feels victimized and put-down). These dialogues always gave me a lift, a shot of creative energy. They became a powerful tool for coping with self-criticism and doubt: an unfailing method for dealing with conflicts of any kind.

As I continued letting my right hand know what my left hand was doing (and vice versa), I could feel the split within me begin to heal. The conscious and unconcsious, the rational and intuitive, the thinking and feeling sides of my inner world began to embrace each other. In times of inner conflict, I turned to this wondrous process. It always brought clarity and insight. It always left me feeling better.

After six months of right/left hand dialogues, I was anxious to share this new discovery with others. My friend, Sally, and I co-directed a one day seminar called *The Creative Woman.* In one activity the group expressed themselves in spontaneous drawings. Then I suggested they write a conversation between Inner Child and Inner Parent using both hands. It was fun, off-beat, and revealing. We were all pleased with the results.

Some time after the workshop, I got a call from one of the participants, Mary. She was an attractive woman in her forties with a dry wit and a ready willingness to try new things. At the time, Mary was a nurse and had just completed training in Marriage, Family, and Child Counseling. She also had three grown daughters and was married to a scientist from the California Institute of Technology in Pasadena. Here is what Mary told me:

> After your *Creative Woman* workshop where I wrote with my left hand for the first time in my life, I started writing out dialogues with my Inner Child. I knew the theory from training in Transactional Analysis, but I didn't really experience it viscerally until I did these dialogues in my own journal.
>
> Well! That Little Child was a source of wild amazement for me. What I discovered was that she had been so squashed down it was a wonder that she was alive at all.
>
> My feelings started pouring out, gushing up like a geyser. I started changing—fast. I became spontaneous, expressive, emotional, and more creative.
>
> A little while after your workshop, we went to a Cal Tech faculty party where I had a conversation with Roger Sperry. You know, he has done the major brain research showing the special functions of each hemisphere. I told him about your workshop and that you had us writing with our non-dominant hands. Since continuing to write with my left hand my behavior had changed. *I* was changing. I was becoming a more spontaneous, more expressive, more feeling person. As a brain researcher, did he make any connections? I was really curious. I knew a little about the brain/body connection: that the right hemisphere of the brain controls the left side of the body, and the left hemisphere controls the right side.
>
> Yes, he did see the connections: "You're opening up your right hemisphere," Roger Sperry said.

"And I wanted to let you know about that, Lucia," Mary continued, "because Sperry is probably *the* expert in brain research. You might want to look into all this, to know more about what you've already discovered. I think you may have stumbled onto something that's much bigger than you think."

I was fascinated by Mary's story and by Roger Sperry's observation. (Several years later, in 1981, Roger Sperry received a Nobel Prize for his pioneering research into the hemispheric functions of the human brain.) Until that conversation with Mary, I had made no connection between the scientific theory and my right/left hand writing experiences. I had heard a little bit about the brain research, but had forgotten all about it.

Thoroughly delighted that Mary had discovered new qualities in herself through writing with her other hand, my mind was flooded with a million thoughts and questions. Was Mary right? Had I stumbled onto something significant? Could writing with the *other hand* benefit others as much as it had me? What did hand dominance have to do with brain function? Hanging up the phone, I sat staring at my left hand on the receiver. At that moment in time, I first glimpsed the magnitude of my discovery: *the power hidden in the other hand.*

Shortly after that conversation, I changed careers and became an art therapist, specializing in what I called the Creative Journal. I taught structured activities for keeping a personal growth journal or diary through drawing and writing with both hands. Since 1974, I have introduced writing with the other hand to thousands of people of all ages and backgrounds. This field work has been the basis of my research and has provided the raw material for this book. I have observed people using these techniques and becoming more creative, expressive, intuitive in their lives. It is not unusual for people to experience more productivity in their work and greater fulfillment in their relationships. I have seen people improve their health and develop inner healing powers. Many contact their spiritual source, or what I refer to in this book as the Inner Self.

The exercises in this book have all been field-tested with groups and individual clients, both in my practice as an Art Therapist and in my journal workshops and support groups. You'll find exercises which will help you

deal with feelings in a safe, healthy, productive way

uncover hidden artistic abilities

discover the playful spirit so essential to the creative process

release old emotions stored in parts of the body

change negative attitudes about yourself

heal your relationships with others

contact a higher power (some call it the Higher Self) greater than your own personality or ego.

The methods presented here are not substitutes for treatment by a physician or health professional. If you are ill or suffering from a chronic problem, consult with your doctor or other health professional.

My goal in writing this book is not to explain the origins of handedness in humans. Scientists and academicians run circles around themselves trying to answer these questions. Questions like: What causes hand dominance? Why are most people right-handed? What does the hand dominance have to do with brain function? I will share briefly what I discovered about handedness and the phenomenon of right-hand dominance passed down through the centuries. We'll look at myths and meanings surrounding right and left and the historical/cultural conspiracy against the left (including the left hand).

In my historical research, the thing that struck me was *the all-pervasive conspiracy against the left hand.* I believe that this conspiracy reflects man's fear of what the left has come to represent: "the other," the feminine, the dark, the unknown, the non-rational, the weak, the primitive, the Child Within. No matter how much education we've had, no matter how verbal or left-brain we are, no matter how intellectual, logical or organized, we still have that "other side" within.

As members of a so-called advanced society, we are taught to place a higher value on the "civilized," rational, adult self. We look down upon the qualities of the "other side"—the intuitive, emotional, artistic, poetic, child-like, and non-rational. So here we have a civil war within the psyche—a split mind (schizophrenia).

This book was born out of my own personal struggle with this "battle of the psyche." When my left hand was allowed to "speak" for the first time, I heard the voice of a long-forgotten self, a part of me that cried out for attention, that longed to be listened to. It eventually brought me to my Inner Self, the Divine Spirit or Higher Power that lives within all of us dressed in the costume of our personalities.

GUIDELINES

Before you venture forth on this journey, I'd like to offer some simple but necessary guidelines. First, in doing the writing and drawing activities in this book, it is important that you *find or create a private place* free from noise, distractions, and outer demands. This work requires concentraion and an atmosphere conducive to self-reflection. You will also need to *make enough time* to do it without hurry or pressure. To get the most out of each exercise, allow yourself fifteen to thirty-minutes of uninterrupted time.

It is advisable to read this book one chapter at a time, digesting the material and doing each activity before going on. Or your style may be to skim the entire book first to get an overview, reading it and then going back doing the exercises. Just don't expect to read and do all the exercises in one sitting.

You will need to prepare yourself by gathering some simple materials:

two pens (ballpoint or felt pens) or two pencils

colored felt pens (8 to 12 assorted colors)

unlined paper 8½" × 11" or larger. Your choice of plain white bond, an artist's spiral-bound sketch pad, or three-ring folder with unlined paper, your own personal diary or journal.

The important thing to remember is that your work is highly personal and should therefore be kept *confidential.* You do not have to share it with the world. Some of these exercises may bring up sensitive issues or feelings and you don't want to subject yourself to the scrutiny and analysis of others. For this reason, you may want to keep your work in a safe, private place away from critical eyes and unsympathetic minds.

On the other hand, you may want to share some of your insights with someone you really trust, such as a therapist or loved one who is non-judgmental with regard to your personal expressions. Use discretion and be selective. Above all, make it safe for yourself to do this work.

I hope the journey you are about to begin will be rewarding and will enable you to find the power that lies hidden in your *other hand.*

CHAPTER ONE

In My Own Hands

How should we be able to forget those ancient myths that are at the beginning of all peoples, the myths about dragons that at the last moment turn into princesses; perhaps all the dragons of our lives are princesses who are only waiting to see us once beautiful and brave. Perhaps everything terrible is in its deepest being something helpless that wants help from us.

—Rainer Maria Rilke
Letters to a Young Poet

My days in seclusion were as somber and gray as the skies that summer of 1973. The famous sunshine of Southern California could only be found in the large quantities of orange juice I was consuming then. The fog near the Santa Monica shore had become the perfect metaphor for my own bleak condition. I was bedridden for three months with a mysterious malaise. It first appeared as complete physical exhaustion very much like the symptoms of mononucleosis. Initial lab tests ruled that out. The ensuing months of tests and prescribed medications turned into a horrible black comedy of medical errors.

At the time I belonged to a health plan which provided its own doctors, clinics, and hospital care. I went to one of the outpatient clinics and saw a physician who talked of viruses and prescribed antibiotics to prevent further complications. My next lab test results were mixed up with those of another patient, and I was given a prescription for the wrong medication. After that I was plagued with infections (vaginal, bladder, and sinus) accompanied by bouts with insomnia, headaches, depression, and anxiety attacks.

While spending hours in waiting rooms being directed from one specialist to another, I began to feel that the medical treatment I was receiving was life-threatening in itself. During this time, my new "friend" and constant companion was the personal journal I began keeping at the onset of the illness. One journal entry gave voice to my true thoughts and feelings:

> *Doctors' offices:*
>
> *Cold—colorless impersonal—wordy—intellectual—intimidating.*
>
> *"I'm broken, doctor, fix me." Probe, harshness, some pain. "Here's what's wrong." (I don't understand fully, ask for causes, he doesn't know but acts as if he does—in a know-it-all manner.)*
>
> *"Here, take these three times a day . . ." I have put so many poisons in my body. Pills, capsules, ointments, suppositories, injections, etc., etc. They relieve the pain but cause more illness. Killing sterilizing healthy organisms. . . .*
>
> *I have been medicated to death.*

Seven years later I saw Dr. Wheelright, a health-care professional trained in the ancient Chinese method of diagnosis called Iridology. In this system, the doctor reads markings and colorings in the irises of the eyes in order to determine past and current physical conditions. At a glance, he accurately recited my entire health history, from my earliest years on. He looked me right in the eye and asked, "When you were thirty-five, did you come unglued?" I answered with a big, "Yes. How did you know?" He told me I had had a collagen disease, similar to what Norman Cousins experienced and described in his book, *Anatomy of an Illness*. In simple terms, this disease involves the breakdown of the connective tissue or collagen in the body. I flashed back to the pictures I had drawn in my journal while I was sick.

This journal drawing, entitled "Coping with Crisis," was done shortly after I entered therapy in the fall of 1973. It was a purely intuitive yet

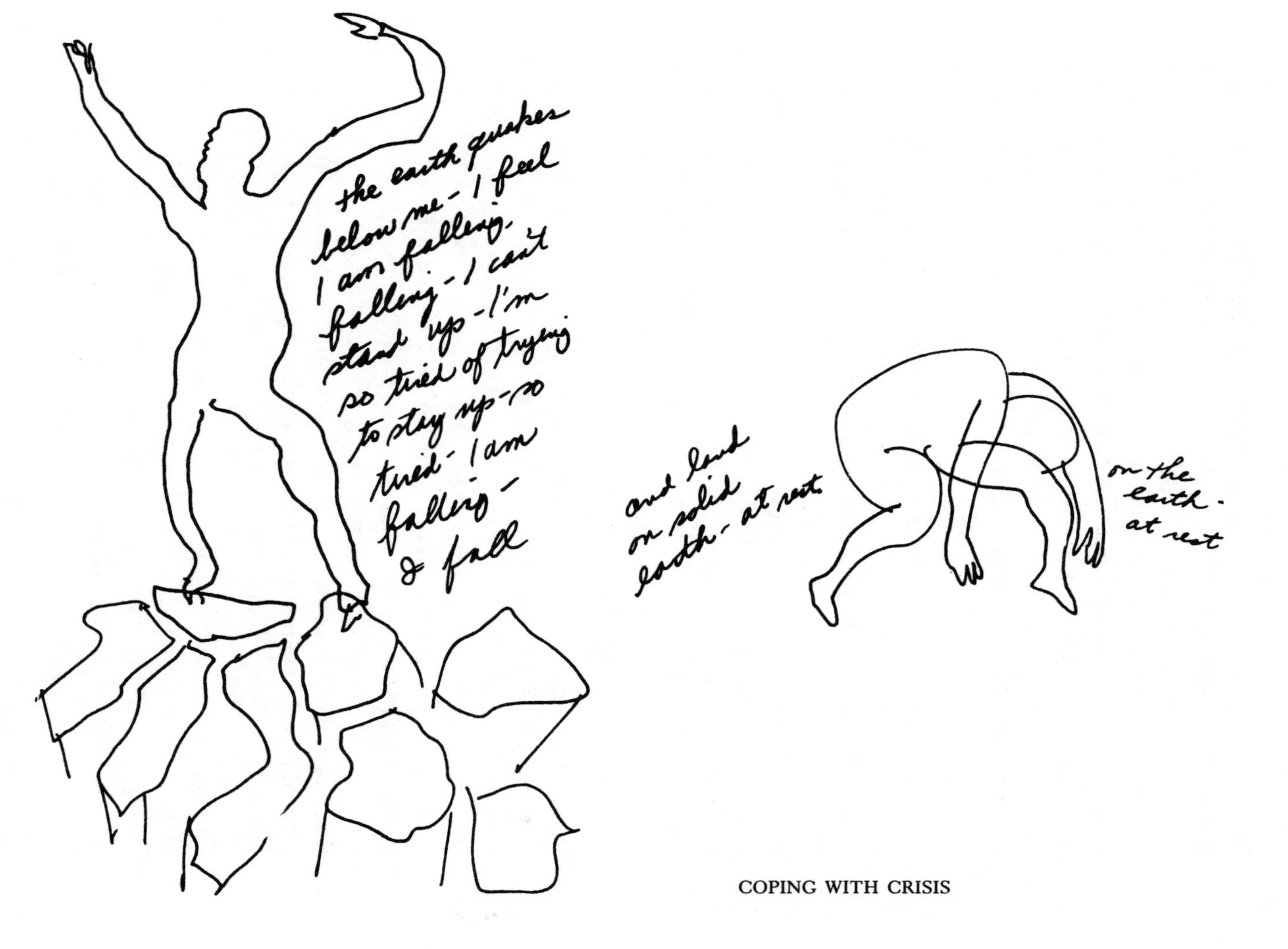

COPING WITH CRISIS

accurate portrayal of my physical condition at that time. My body was coming apart, just as the earth was cracking apart in the drawing. This symbolic representation of my state also showed "the cure" in the form of the fallen figure on the right. My healing really started when I accepted and expressed my feelings of child-like helplessness and fear in the journal. This enabled me to seek out some nurturing and wise individuals who helped me heal and give birth to my new self. Bond Wright, my therapist; Louise Hunt, a nurse trained in accupresure massage; and Dr. Louis Light, a physician practicing preventive medicine.

This journal drawing marked a turning point in my illness. It ushered in a period of intense self-discovery and healing. It turned on the light bulb of awareness by illuminating the meaning of the disease. The drawing was a map to the path of recovery. It showed me that it was time to stop what I had been doing and begin again. I had been under great stress for five years prior to the illness: divorce, relocation, illness of family members, survival as a single parent, and frequent job changes in free-lance work. It is no accident that the fallen figure is in a fetal or child-like position. Surrendering to the needs of my sick body and emotions led to healing and rebirth.

In the introduction I told about how my therapist first put me in touch with my little Inner Child by placing a kindergarten crayon in my left hand and saying, "Write." Several weeks after that experience, another important breakthrough happened. This time I was alone, writing and drawing in the journal with my right hand. Obsessed with finding new meaning for my life after so many critical changes, I had a vague recognition that I needed to change careers, but didn't know in which direction to go.

In the journal, I was describing my recent birthday celebration. A few friends had taken me out for dinner. We returned home and opened the door of my darkened house. All the lights suddenly went on and a huge crowd of people jumped out yelling, "*Happy Birthday!*" The event mirrored the inner rebirth I'd been experiencing. Here is what I wrote and drew in the journal:

RIGHT HAND:

IT WAS HARD WORK. IT *IS* HARD WORK
BEING BORN. AND I DID IT. I'M DOING IT
MYSELF. MY STRENGTH. MINE. IT
IT BELONGS TO ME. *IS* ME. NOW
I GOT WELL. I FIGURED OUT HOW
TO DO IT. WHO TO SEE. HOW
ASK FOR HELP. WHO TO TRUST. WHO TO
WHO TO STAY AWAY FROM. THAT'S
IT. TAKING CARE OF MYSELF
DOESN'T MEAN MAKIN $20,000 A
YEAR. IT MEANS KNOWING
WHERE TO GET STROKES WHEN
I NEED THEM. WHO TO AVOID
THAT HURTS ME. HOW TO GET
WHAT I WANT. KNOW WHAT
I WANT. EXPRESS IT.

RIGHT HAND:

As I wrote the words, A *new life from the old,* a critical voice whispered in my head: "Yes, but you'd better hurry up. You've been searching too long."

Then something clicked inside, like shifting gears. Suddenly my left hand grabbed the pen out of my right hand. My Little Child Within wrote and drew a picture of herself for the first time. She "answered back" to the judgmental Critical Parent that was chattering in my mind. She asserted herself against that insidious voice that was gnawing away at my self-confidence. *The Inner Child started it all: my first left hand/right hand dialogue.*

LEFT HAND:

LEFT HAND: WHY ARE YOU SO IMPATIENT

RIGHT HAND: Because I'm tired of waiting - feels like sitting in a rut -

LEFT HAND: BUT LOOK AT THE PAINTINGS WE'VE DONE · LIKE NOTHING THAT WENT BEFORE -

RIGHT HAND: I know but it seems like so little. I feel so ignorant when I look around - all those other designers with all that technical skill - THIS IS PIG PARENT SPEAKING · YOU'RE SO STUPID - UNPROFFESSIONAL CAN'T DO PERSPECTIVE DRAWING - DO SAME OLD

RIGHT HAND: THING - MOVE - GODDAMMIT MOVE - DO SOMETHING NEW - I WANT TO SHAKE YOU - HURRY UP

LEFT HAND: I HATE YOU WHEN YOU DO THIS - STOP PUTTING ME DOWN - STOP

LEFT HAND:

I'M
BEAUTIFUL
AND
MY BEAUTY
GROWS
AND
GROWS
AND
MY STRENGTH
GROWS
I AM ALWAYS GROWING UP

THERE'S NOTHING THAT CAN STOP ME

OBSERVATION BY RIGHT HAND:

Sitting in a nest feels like
being shut in - in the dark -
in the womb - waiting to be
born into the light - waiting
until the time comes
naturally - not forcing,
not pushing - just relaxing
and letting life happen
and letting me happen
naturally

How liberating! In that dialogue I realized I had found the key to unlock a power within myself. This power could help me deal with the demons of self-criticism and doubt. That dialogue took me back to childhood, when I was brain-washed with a litany of put-downs recited by the grown-ups. "You're not working hard enough. . . . You're lazy . . . . You're messy. . . . You're awkward. . . . Your grades aren't good enough. . . ."

That dialogue showed me exactly how I was still replaying the external Critical Parent messages recorded in my brain during childhood. Those messages were still putting me down. It all added up to one thing: *No matter how much you accomplish, it's never good enough.* Through the right/left hand dialogue I got to know the child I was before learning those negative attitudes. Now I could talk with her at any time in my journal. I didn't have to wait until my next therapy session. That Inner Child who "spoke" through my *other hand* turned out to be a source of strength I'd had all along, but had lost somewhere in the business of growing up.

Later I had other dialogues: with body parts needing to be healed, emotions wanting to be released, dreams yearning to see the light of day, creative ideas wanting to be born, and inner wisdom giving me answers to life's questions. A whole cast of "characters" spoke through my *other hand*, as well: a frightened Vulnerable Child; a silly Playful Kid; an outrageous Woman in Red; an Inner Healer; a serene Wise Woman. I encountered the archetypes of which the renowned Swiss psychologist C. G. Jung wrote: The Great Mother, the Old Wise Man, the Trickster, the Goddess. I even wrote out conversations with other people in my life. But most important of all, my *other hand* led me to my Inner Self or God Within—that source of love, peace, and wisdom which we all possess as our human birthright and which we can contact directly.

And now let me introduce you to your *other hand.* Since writing with the non-dominant hand is usually difficult for beginners, you will start out by writing something you know very well: your name. You will then have a chance to express any frustrations and judgments you have about writing with your *other hand.* Breaking old patterns is often uncomfortable and ego-deflating. This first exercise will probably jostle your ego. It will also help you observe your typical reactions to awkward moments and unfamiliar situations. Just notice what happens.

WRITING WITH THE OTHER HAND

Materials: Unlined paper and a pen or pencil

1. Pick up the pen/pencil with your *other hand* (the hand you don't normally write with).
2. Print or write your name. Don't worry about neatness, legibility, or penmanship.
3. Continue writing with your non-dominant hand. This time print or write how it feels to be writing with this hand. Don't worry about spelling, grammar, syntax, or vocabulary.
4. Read what you wrote. Then switch to your dominant hand and write down your reaction to what you wrote with your *other hand.* How did it feel to do it? What does the handwriting look like to you? What other thoughts or feelings come up? How did you react to doing things differently, to experiencing the unknown, the unfamiliar?

As you continue writing with your *other hand,* the initial awkwardness will eventually lessen. Notice any new feelings and insights that emerge.

LEFT HAND:

I'M WRITING THIS WITH
MY LEFT HAND. IT IS
VERY HARD TO DO.
I'M FRUSTRATED
BECAUSE IT'S SO
SLOW. MY THOUGHTS
ARE RACING AHEAD
BUT MY HAND CAN'T
CATCH UP.

CHAPTER TWO

The Upper Hand and the Other Hand

Human beings have two hands.
One hand is called dominant, the other has no name.
One hand is defined by what it can do, the other by what it cannot do.
One hand is trained and educated, the other is ignored and unschooled.
One hand writes, the other is illiterate.
One hand is skilled, the other is awkward.
One hand is powerful, the other is weak.
No matter which hand is dominant, right or left, the same internal politics exist.
One has the "upper hand," the other is "left out."

I'm going to share with you some biological and cultural explanations of the phenomenon of handedness in humans. Personally, I find the research and theories fascinating. However, if you are yawning at the very thought of reading left-brain historical and theoretical material, just wait. There are pictures and hands-on experiences to keep both sides of your brain entertained.

HANDEDNESS: THE PREFERENCE OF ONE HAND OVER THE OTHER

As far as we know, individual humans have always had a dominant hand. We accept handedness unquestioningly as being "in the nature of things." We expect it to be so and we teach it to our children. As soon as the infant feeds itself or grabs a toy, we encourage or coerce it to prefer one hand. Later, the child scribbles, draws pictures, and eventually learns to write its own name with the dominant hand.

Some people are ambidextrous—up to a point. The line is drawn at writing. Right-handed, left-handed, or ambidextrous, most of us write with only one hand. Early in life a choice is made and sometimes forced by parents or teachers: one hand or the other.

Why is this so? Our hands *look* alike. Why don't they *act* alike, particularly when it comes to writing? Is it simply that specialization is more efficient? Was specialization necessary for the evolutionary leap to the use of tools, language, and symbols? Was functional asymmetry inevitable in the development of homo sapiens? Is imbalance the price we pay for literacy?

RIGHT IS RIGHT: MAJORITY RULE

As if our questions about individual handedness were not enough, we have another curious fact at the social level: we live in a right-handed world. Around the turn of the century, Robert Hertz, an eminent anthropologist, observed:

> . . . in every quarter of the world it is the right hand, and not the left, which is predominant, and this is so whether in the great civilizations of Europe and India or among the most primitive and isolated peoples known. The issue can be studied in such varied fields as the Homeric poems, alchemy, and thirteenth-century French religious art, in Hindu iconography, classical Chinese state ceremonies, emblem books and bestiaries, as well as in Maori ritual, Bornean divination, and the myths of the most disparate cultures.

Although a majority are right-handed, historically this may not have always been so. Stone-Age tools and cave paintings give evidence of a more even distribution of right-handers and left-handers among our ancient ancestors. However, by the Bronze Age the right hand seems to have gotten the upper hand.

In more recent history, there are isolated cases of left-handed cultures. In the Old Testament, King David is said to have been aided by an army of left-handers. Alexander the Great was reported to have found a tribe of left-handed people. In some contemporary primitive cultures there is a relatively higher proportion of left-handers than there are in the rest of the world. Among these are the Hottentots, Bushmen, Pygmies and Bantu of Africa, Aboriginies of Australia, and natives of New Guinea.

Yet the vast majority of humans are considered to be right-handed. Estimates run 90% and higher, according to some cross-cultural studies. But statistics are unreliable, depending on the definition of handedness. Is the dominant hand the one that writes? That uses tools? That throws a ball? That is stronger? That is used more often? Some people are right-handed for some tasks and left-handed for others. Ambidextrous people use both hands interchangeably.

I have worked with another group who have been ignored. I call them *switch-overs,* that is, left-handers who were forced by parents or teachers to write with the right hand. We don't know how many switch-overs there are. Many switch-overs don't even know that they were once naturally left-handed. I encounter such people all the time in my workshops and private practice. When they begin writing with the left hand, they are flooded with childhood memories of early power struggles in which they were forcibly (often cruelly) made to conform to the majority rule. It was indelibly imprinted on their young minds that the *left hand was the wrong hand for writing.* They repressed these experiences long ago and forgot their true handedness. My clinical experience confirms that much psychological damage was done. Often these individuals would have trouble finding my office for their first art therapy session. In private work it would frequently be revealed that they had great difficulty finding their way in life. They chose the "wrong" careers, seemed to be living in unsatisfying relationships and locations. Something very basic had been betrayed at an early age, and it appeared to have long-term effects. However, the techniques presented in this book helped them to revive their natural handedness.

Benjamin Franklin, statesman, philosopher, author, and inventor, was a proponent of eduction for both hands. The following was his serious attempt to recommend ambidextrality to the teaching profession:

A PETITION TO THOSE WHO HAVE THE SUPERINTENDENCY OF EDUCATION

> I address myself to all the friends of youth, and conjure them to direct their compassionate regard to my unhappy fate, in order to remove the prejudices of which I am the victim. There are twins sisters of us; and the eyes of man do not more resemble, nor are capable of being on better terms with each other than my sister and myself, were it not for the partiality of our parents, who made the most injurious distinction between us.
>
> From my infancy I have been led to consider my sister as a being of more educated rank. I was suffered to grow up without the least instruction, while nothing was spared in her education. She had masters to teach her writing, drawing, music, and other accomplishments, but if by chance I touched a pencil, a pen, or a needle I was bitterly rebuked; and more than once I have been beaten for being awkward and wanting a graceful manner.
>
> Must not the regret of our parents be excessive, at having placed so great a difference between sisters who are so perfectly equal? Alas! We must perish from distress; for it would not be in my power even to scrawl a suppliant petition for relief . . . .
>
> Condescend, sir, to make my parents sensible of the injustice of an exclusive tenderness, and of the necessity of distributing their care and affection among all their children equally. I am, with profound respect, Sirs,
>
> Your obedient servant,
>
> THE LEFT HAND

Why would society prefer one hand over another? And why, throughout the world and throughout history, was the right hand chosen as the superior hand?

THEORIES OF HANDEDNESS

In western history, explanations of hand dominance in humans fall into two opposing schools of thought: biological and cultural. As in so many areas of science, the debate between nature vs. nurture applies here, too. For instance, Plato believed we were meant to be balanced (ambidextrous) individuals and that any hand dominance was the result of bad child-rearing habits. Aristotle had a biological point of view and believed right-handedness was due to an inherently greater strength in the right side of the body.

Theories of handedness proliferated through the ages. The following are a few of the more popular explanations for why humans prefer one hand and why it was the right hand that achieved pre-eminence.

BIOLOGICAL THEORIES

THE GENETIC THEORY

Is handedness handed down? Many left-handers come from families in which left-handedness can be traced from one generation to another. A long-standing common belief is that handedness is genetic and explanable by Mendelian laws of heredity. And yet, there is evidence drawn from studies of twins that puts the "inheritance theory" into question. Also, if left-handedness runs in families, couldn't it just as well be a learned habit, as Plato suggested?

VISCERAL DISTRIBUTION THEORY

One notion in vogue in the nineteenth century was the "theory of visceral distribution." It was pointed out that the internal organs of the human body are asymmetrically arranged, with the heavier organs (such as the liver) on the right side. In order to balance ourselves, it was reasoned, we favored the left foot. This allowed the right hand freedom for activity and full development through greater use. Hence homo sapiens evolved into a right-handed species. By this reasoning left-handed people would be "left-livered."

RIGHT/LEFT BRAIN THEORY

The current physiological explanation of handedness is based on brain research into hemispheric functions. We know that the left hemisphere of the brain controls the entire right side of the body; the right hemisphere controls the left side. In the nineteenth century, Paul Broca, a French brain surgeon/neurologist, located a speech center in the left hemisphere of the brain. This small region in the third convolution of the left frontal lobe of the cerebral cortex became known as Broca's Area. Broca concluded from his discovery that "We're right-handed because we're left-brained." Broca also went on to consider the relationship between handedness and speech. He suggested that both speech and manual dexterity are attributable to an inborn superiority of the left hemisphere in right-handers.

Later research revealed other language centers in the left hemisphere. It has been found that 98% of right-handers have language centers in the left hemisphere of the brain. Speech loss (aphasia) results from damage to the left brain. There is also a great deal of evidence linking weakness or paralysis in the right side of the body with speech disturbances and damage to the language centers in the left hemisphere. The exception that proves the rule are the 2% of right-handers who have right-hemisphere language centers. Some researchers suggest this may result from early left brain damage causing the right brain to compensate and develop language abilities.

One would expect left-handers to be the opposite of right-handers, that is, with language centers in the right brain. It turns out that this is not the case. A two-thirds majority of left-handers have language centers in the left brain, the same as right-handers. Only one-third of left-handed people have language centers in the right side of the brain. We don't know why this is so.

ILLUSTRATION OF HAND/BRAIN DOMINANCE.

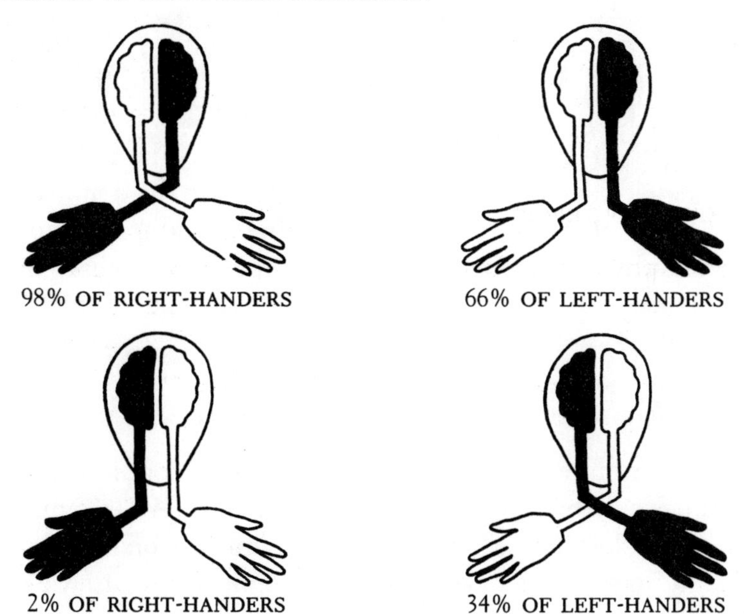

CULTURAL THEORIES

From another point of view, anthropologists and historians have emphasized that cultural factors foster right-handedness.

SUN WORSHIP

One theory about the origins of hand dominance revolves around early sun worship, which was once common throughout the world. When humans in the northern hemisphere face the sun, its path seems to travel from left to right. Supposedly, this caused the tendency toward rightward motion called "clockwise" and explains our preference for the right hand. One would then expect that cultures south of the equator, where the sun appears to move from right to left, would be predominantly left-handed. Although there are a few such contemporary cultures, as mentioned earlier, in which there is a more even distribution of left- and right-handedness, most cultures in the southern hemisphere are predominantly right-handed.

THE HAND THAT WIELDS THE SWORD

Another notion about the cause of right-handedness was the "sword and shield theory" put forth by nineteenth-century historian/essayist Thomas Carlyle, among others. In battle, the shield was held by the left hand protecting the heart and other vital organs. The right hand was trained to wield the sword or weapon, so it became the dominant hand. But how does this account for left-handedness, and more importantly the handedness of the other half of the population, i.e., women who were weaving cloth and rocking the cradle instead of wielding the sword in battle?

DUALISTIC THINKING: RIGHT IS RIGHT, LEFT IS WRONG

In the early twentieth century, German anthropologist Robert Hertz turned Broca's theory on its head. Broca had said, "We're right-handed because we're left-brained." Broca was examining brains. Hertz examined cultures and concluded, "We're left-brained because we're right-handed."

He based his theory on observations of historical beliefs and judgments about right and left. In his now classic essay entitled, "The Pre-eminence of the Right Hand: A Study in Religious Polarity," Hertz declared that dualistic thinking down through the ages had resulted in humanity's preference for the right hand. He reminded us that humans had always believed in right and wrong, good vs. bad. He was the first to hypothesize that these judgments were projected onto the world in terms of spatial relationships: right became the good side, left became the bad. This dualistic thinking was internalized as well: God was put in the right hand, the Devil was placed in the left. In this way, the right hand was given pre-eminence. It got the "upper hand."

Like Benjamin Franklin, Hertz had a passionate concern about injustices against the left hand. This is eloquently expressed in the introduction to his essay:

> What resemblance more perfect than between our two hands! And yet what a striking inequality there is!

> To the right hand go honors, flattering designation, prerogatives: it acts, orders, and it *takes*. The left hand, on the contrary, is despised and reduced to the role of a humble auxiliary: by itself it can do nothing; it helps, it supports, it *holds*.
>
> The right hand is the symbol and model of all aristocracies, the left hand of the plebeians.
>
> What are the titles of the nobility of the right hand? And whence comes the servitude of the left?

A *moral judgment* was made in favor of the right hand. This led to a preference for using the right hand, which in turn led to the greater development of the left hemisphere. It had been proven that the left hemisphere of the brain weighs more than the right hemisphere. From a cultural/environmental perspective, Hertz reasoned:

> It is a known fact that the exercise of an organ leads to greater nourishment and consequently growth of that organ. The greater activity of the right hand, which involves more intensive work for the left nervous centers, has the necessary effect of favoring its development.

Hertz's brilliant work and pioneering support of ambidextrality ended with his death at age thirty-three in World War I. The significance of his work was that he inspired other anthropologists to do cross-cultural research into the attitudes and concepts about right and left. Their findings? Hertz was right. The social scientists found that the same moral judgments and values about right and left were reflected in customs, artifacts, and languages all over the world. It is quite remarkable that among cultures separated by both time and distance, agreement seems to exist: right is good, left is bad.

The following are three cultural examples showing this phenomenon.

THE MERU TRIBE OF KENYA, AFRICA

RIGHT	LEFT
north	south
white clans	black clans
day	night
senior	junior
dominant age-division	subordinate age-division
man	woman
superior	inferior
east	west
sunrise	sunset
sun	——(moon?)
light	darkness
sight (eyes)	blindness

MAPUCHE (CHILE, SOUTH AMERICA)

RIGHT	LEFT
good	evil
life	death
day	night
health	sickness
ancestral spirits	*wekufe* (evil spirits)
shaman	sorcerer
afterworld	underworld
abundance	poverty
fullness	hunger

ENGLISH LANGUAGE DICTIONARY AND THESAURUS

RIGHT		LEFT	LEFT-HANDED
correct	straight	clumsy	crippled
direct	true	awkward	defective
equitable	unswerving	insincere	underhanded dealing
duty	upright	indirect	ambiguous
fair	virtuous	weak	doubtful
good		worthless	questionable
honest		gauche	ill-omened
just		sinister	inauspicious
lawful			sinister
perpendicular			unpropitious
privilege			
rightful			

THE CONSPIRACY AGAINST THE LEFT HAND

Perhaps there is a biological tendency toward left-brain/right-hand dominance, as physiological research indicates. But why have humans the world over attached *moral and social values* to right and left? With the exception of classical Chinese culture and some American Indian tribes, it appears that this belief—*right is superior, left is inferior*—is one thing almost all of humanity has agreed upon, regardless of race, religion, geographical location, or historical period. *That* is remarkable in itself.

Over the centuries, there appears to have been a conspiracy. We have done more than ignore the left hand, we have actually abused it. In the myths and customs of many peoples: *Left is bad and right is good.* These include Hindus, Arabs, the Maori of New Zealand, the Mojave and Chipewa Indians of America, and many African tribes. In numerous cultures the left hand is considered "dirty" and is reserved for "unclean acts" of a personal nature, such as wiping away excrement. Along with this are taboos forbidding the left hand to perform "clean" or social acts, such as preparing and cooking food, eating, and greeting. In some cultures, the left hand and arm are mutilated in ritual practice.

The left hand fares no better in so-called advanced, literate societies. It is common for parents and teachers to force left-handed children to write with the right hand. Many of my naturally left-handed students and private clients have told me how they were ridiculed, physically restrained, or punished for writing with the "wrong hand." After repeatedly having their left hand slapped or tied down, some of these individuals finally gave up and switched over to the majority hand. They feel, and I agree, that deep psychological damage was done. Is this a modern-day version of physical mutilation of the left hand practiced by so-called primitives?

Since the French Revolution, the terms left-wing and right-wing have come to stand for opposing political factions. These labels originated with the seating arrangements of the French National Assembly in the eighteenth century. The conservatives sat on the presiding officer's right, the radical revolutionaries sat on his left, and the moderates were placed across from him in the center. Considering the values placed on right and left by humanity in general, it is no accident that the opposing groups were positioned as they were in relation to the center. Even in modern times, it is the left wing that becomes the object of political witch-hunts, as in the McCarthy Era.

In folklore, the left hand definitely has a bad name. Witches were said to be left-handed. In everyday conversation today terms like "left-handed compliment" and "out in left field" have negative connotations. It is worth noting here that in diverse cultures the left side is associated with the feminine principle. In eastern traditions, the left side of the body is considered feminine or receptive, as opposed to the active right side. In heraldry, the feminine side of one's ancestry is pictured on the left side of the coat of arms. Even today, in Christian wedding ceremonies, the bride's family and friends are seated on the left upon entering the church, while the groom's side is on the right.

We shape our language and our language in turn shapes us. As a human creation, language both forms and reflects our perceptions, beliefs and values. Nowhere is this seen more clearly than in the origins and meanings of the words *left* and *left-handed* in modern languages. Notice the striking similarity and the common prejudice against the "sinistral" side.

ENGLISH DERIVATION FOR *LEFT*

LANGUAGE	WORD	MEANING
Kentish form of	lyft	weak
	lyftade	paralysis
Anglo-Saxon	lefan (v)	to leave; be left
	laf (n)	what is left, remnants, left-overs, inheritance

LANGUAGE	WORD FOR LEFT	OTHER MEANINGS
Hindi	Khabba labra	weakness, dishonor
Arab	usrawi	weakness, dishonor
Turkish	solak	weakness, dishonor
Russian	lievia	weakness, dishonor
Chinese	young tso show teih	
	tso	counter, oppose
German	das linksseyn link	someone awkward
French	gauche	(orig. meaning—bent)
English	gauche	clumsy, awkward
	gawky (slang)	clumsy, awkward
	sinister	evil
Saxon	winstre	evil
Danish	venstre	evil
Swedish	wanstre	evil

LANGUAGE	WORD FOR LEFT	OTHER MEANINGS
Icelandic	vinstri	evil
Spanish	zurdo (left-handed)	malicious, going in the wrong direction
	non se zurdo	"Don't be stupid."
Italian	mancini	defective, maimed deceitful (from *mancus*—maimed)
	stanca (left-handedness)	fatigued
Portuguese	conhoto (left-handedness)	weak, mischievous
Russian	leja (left-hander)	(insult), sneakiness
Romany (Gypsy language)	bongo (left-hand)	evil, crooked

Obviously, the left hand does not have very good press. It is surrounded by a general air of suspicion, fear, or outright condemnation. In all the references to right and left in the Bible, according to one scholar, "In no single instance is the left hand given a position of honor, superiority or righteousness." (Ponder the very word: *right*eousness.) The Old Testament says that "The right hand of the Lord hath pre-eminence." (Psalms 118:16) It is also interesting to note that Michelangelo's God used his right hand to confer life upon Adam. Observe also that Adam received the gift of life with his left hand.

ADAM RECEIVING LIFE FROM GOD

YIN/YANG SYMBOL

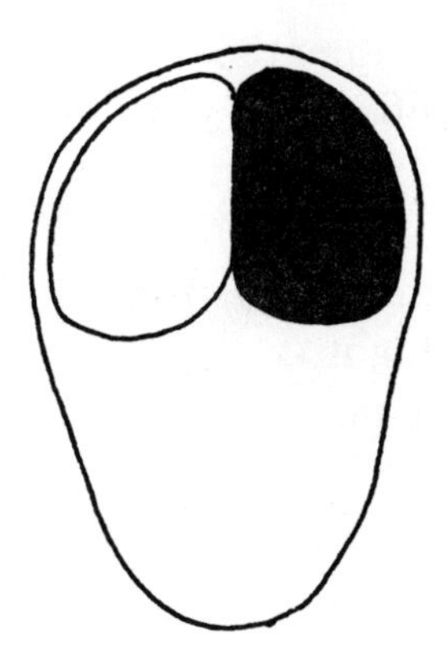

TWO HEMISPHERES OF THE HUMAN BRAIN

Below is a list of polarities gathered by noted researcher Robert Ornstein.

SOURCE	RIGHT	LEFT
Many sources	Day	Night
Blackburn	Intellectual	Sensual
Oppenheimer	Time, History	Eternity, Timelessness
Deikman	Active	Receptive
Polanyi	Explicit	Tacit
Levy, Sperry	Analytic	Gestalt
Domhoff	Right (side of body)	Left (side of body)
Many sources	Left Hemisphere	Right Hemisphere
Bogen	Propositional	Appositional
Lee	Lineal	Nonlineal
Luria	Sequential	Simultaneous
Semmes	Focal	Diffuse
I Ching	The Creative: heaven masculine, Yang	The Receptive: earth feminine, Yin
I Ching	Light	Dark
I Ching	Time	Space
Many sources	Verbal	Spatial
Many sources	Intellectual	Intuitive
Vedanta	Buddhi	Manas
Jung	Causal	Acausal
Bacon	Argument	Experience

Below are the most common descriptions from students who have just written with both the dominant hand (the Write Hand) and the *other hand.*

THE WRITE HAND	THE OTHER HAND
legible	illegible
familiar	sloppy
controlled	awkward
precise	strange
fast	slow
dexterity	embarrassing
skilled	frustrating
correct	unfamiliar
follows rules	child-like
intellect	emotional
conscious	unconscious
polite	unruly
rational	intuitive
cerebral	gutsy
mental	feeling
self-righteous	direct
critical	poetic
judgmental	flowing
stiff	spontaneous
proper	errors
neat	reversal of letters
longer words	short, simple words
round about	to the point

The next activity will help you personalize what you've read about the human brain and about polarities. You'll be picturing your own brain and describing in words what your own experience is. You'll be exercising both sides of your brain, the visual/spatial/imaginative right brain and the verbal left brain. For this exercise, I suggest you use colored pens.

TWO SIDES OF THE BRAIN

1. Draw a picture of your head showing both sides of the brain. (See the illustration below for an example.)
2. Starting with your right brain (on the left side of the picture), portray it through color, pattern, or images. What kind of energy do you feel there? Is it heavy or light? Quiet or busy? Dark or light?
3. Repeat the process, this time showing your left brain (on the right side of your picture).
4. When you've completed your drawing, write a description of each side.

The right side of my brain feels smooth, bright, engorged. It pulsates with energy. Through the undulating hills and valleys the energy flows with a slow, steady deliberate beat. (Colors: red, orange, and yellow.)

The left side of my brain feels bumpy, fuzzy with electric energy zip-zapping in all directions. It may *seem* smaller in size but the energy zipping all over creates an "aura" surrounding this side—so actually both sides *are* the same size. (Colors: gray, pink dots, blue straight lines.)

It is a balanced brain—although both halves are different.

5. Now try your hand at writing with your *other hand.* This will be your opportunity to respond to what you've read so far about the history and origins of handedness and the cultural attitudes about the left and the right. It will help to personalize the information and make the experience relevant to your own life and experiences.

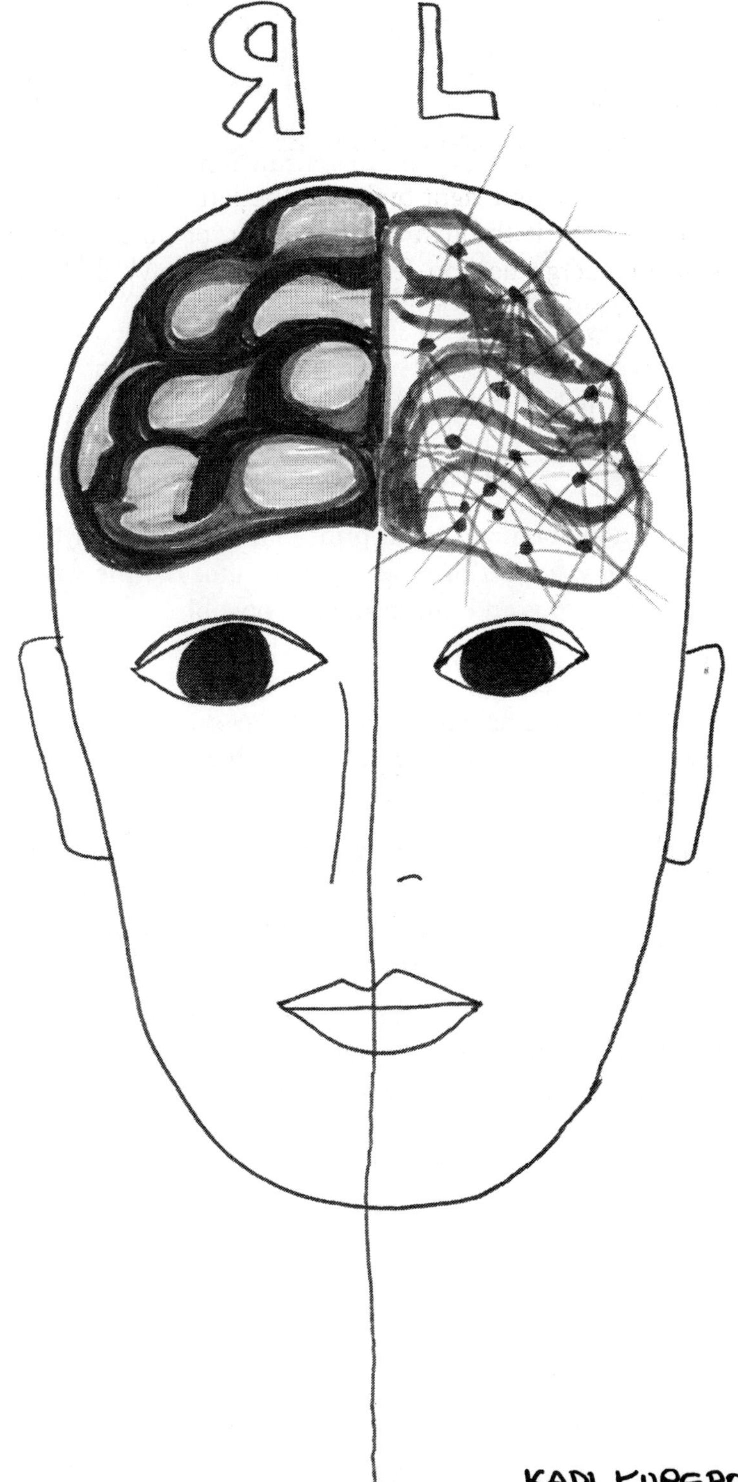
R L
KADI KURGPOLD 7-26-80

TÊTE-À-TÊTE

> With your non-dominant hand, print or write any thoughts and responses you have to what you've read so far. Does anything you've read correspond to your own life? If so, what?

Now that you've gotten your own thoughts and feelings flowing out, this may be a time when your initial uneasiness about writing with the other hand begins to subside. If so, feel free to continue by writing on any topic of your choice. Watch for new feelings or intuitions. See where your writing leads.

OFF THE TOP OF MY HEAD

> Let your non-dominant hand print or write about anything you wish, any subject or aspect of your life. Let the writing be as spontaneous and uncensored as possible.

Did you notice any change in the way you expressed yourself? This could be a time when a new personality or flavor comes through. If so, it is probably a shift from a more rational, left-brain style to a more sensitive and emotional right-brain one.

Do you notice any difference in expression between your "normal" dominant handwriting and this new way to write? Do you say things differently? Is there a stylistic difference in terms of word usage, grammar, content? If so, describe them.

CHAPTER THREE

Letting the Right Hand Know What the Left Hand Is Doing

The great Tao flows everywhere, both to the left and to the right.

—Tao Te Ching

THE POLITICS OF THE HANDS

In teaching hundreds of people to write with both hands, I've observed over and over that writing done with the *other hand* often expresses the disowned and oppressed parts of the self. With profound simplicity the *other hand* speaks for the powerless, weak, subordinate aspect of the personality. This "silent partner" releases emotions and desires which have been stored away in the unconscious. You may wonder why this is so. The non-dominant hand is generally considered the *wrong* hand for writing, so it is the *perfect* hand for expressing anything in ourselves which has been judged as wrong.

Writing with the *other hand* brings up feelings of awkwardness. It is the unschooled hand. Since it has not been trained to write, its handwriting looks like a child's: slow, awkward, clumsy, ugly (by most standards of penmanship). Often the scrawls are barely legible. Spelling errors frequently occur, even among good spellers.

Almost all the people I've worked with said they felt child-like and vulnerable when they first wrote or printed with the *other hand.* Some people report that primitive and raw emotions came to the surface. The Inner Child frequently comes out in a rush of feeling. And beneath the layers of hidden emotions, one finds an intuitive and creative voice. When you realize that the non-dominant hand is governed by the right hemisphere in most people, it is no surprise that the qualities ascribed to the right brain—creative, emotional, intuitive—are precisely the qualities that come out most easily when the non-dominant hand writes. You will see this in illustrations and examples throughout this book.

It is easier to express feelings by writing with the *other hand.* For that reason, it is an excellent therapeutic technique. Scribbling out rage, fear, frustrations, sadness, helplessness, and vulnerability can bring immeasurable relief, both physically and emotionally. It's a wonderful way to reduce stress caused by a build-up of emotions. It's a safe method for letting off steam without hurting anyone or anything. It's a playful way to dump emotions without attacking others or the environment.

There is energy and life in feelings. The energy doesn't go away simply because those feelings are denied or stuffed down. On the contrary, the bottled-up energy turns rancid and becomes pain, depression, or disease. Thwarted emotions may eventually erupt in verbal outbursts or physical violence. Writing or drawing with the *other hand* allows feelings to come safely to the surface to be acknowledged and accepted.

Each of us can contribute to a more peaceful world by taking responsibility for our own feelings of violence and by defusing our personal artillery of emotional explosives. We do this when we face our feelings and accept them instead of hiding from them. There are many ways to do this safely and productively: playing with clay, scribbling or drawing, beating up some pillows, doing physical excercise or sports, dancing, yelling, singing, or writing.

I have received numerous thank-you notes and calls from people who have successfully vented difficult emotions by writing with the *other hand.* The following incident demonstrates the values of this technique when used in stressful situations. One of my clients, Janet, used left-hand writing to save her job. How? By expressing powerful emotions which, if mishandled, would have led to untimely dismissal from her job.

> *I was at work one day, hating my clerical job and wishing I could be anyplace else. I wanted to be teaching school, which was the new career I was training to enter. We were understaffed that day and my boss was complaining again*

for the umpteenth time about our not getting the work out on schedule.

All my weeks of growing impatience to get out of clerical work and get on with my career as a teacher just seemed to explode inside me. Suddenly, I got so mad I wanted to go in there and strangle my boss. You know, really tell him off. All I could think of was yelling and screaming at the top of my lungs, although I didn't do it.

Something told me to call my therapist, Lucia. I'd just started seeing her a few weeks before. She'd been helping me face up to a lot of feelings I was used to burying under a pleasant, "good girl" exterior. Anger was one of the "biggies." But now I felt trapped. O.K. So I was feeling my anger at the time it came up, but what was I supposed to do with it? It wanted to come out, but strangling my boss didn't seem to be the answer.

I ran out to the pay phone so no one in the office could hear me and called my therapist. Thank God, she answered the phone. I told her about my dilemma, almost blaming her for my predicament. After all, she was the one who was coaching me to feel my feelings. "Do you want to quit your job?" she asked. "No!" I shouted in a whisper. I didn't want anyone in the office to know I was having this conversation. "I can't handle that. I've got finals coming up at school and I've got to have a job. I don't have the time or the energy to go look for another job right now and I've got bills to pay. You know I'm supporting myself." I was getting really agitated. How could she suggest that I quit?

"O.K.," she replied. "That's fine. Now, here's what you do. Go into the ladies' room. Do you have your journal with you? Good. Go in there. What? It's a large restroom with lots of stalls? That's O.K. Go lock yourself into one of the stalls. Sit down and write out all the things you'd really like to do and say to your boss. EVERYTHING. O.K.? And write it with your other hand. *Remember I told you about this technique in one*

of our sessions? Use your left *hand and don't try to be neat or legible. And DON'T be polite. Just let it out.*

I laughed and whispered, "You mean, like taking a good shit?" "Yes," she chuckled. "Exactly."

So I did it. I scrawled pages and pages of it. And, boy what a relief! I called him every name in the book. I told him he should be strung up and so on and so forth. I wrote so fast and furiously, I couldn't even read it afterward. But it worked. I was able to go back to my desk and get things done.

I felt so much better. I wasn't ready to quit. And if I'd had a tantrum like the one I was fantasizing about, he would have fired me on the spot, or else he would have been dead from strangulation and I'd be in jail. I wasn't ready to leave my job at that time. I left a few months later, when I was good and ready. *And I left on good terms. After all, I needed good references. And I got them.*

Janet's experience began as a common struggle with "difficult" feelings. It turned into a victory over the tyranny of buried emotions which could have exploded in a way that would have been counterproductive to her personal goals: to stay employed at her job until she *chose* to leave.

Do you have an authority figure or petty tyrant in your life, such as a boss, parent, teacher, or mate? If you do, now is the time to let out your feelings in a private and safe place. The outcome may lead to a shift in your attitude and a way of perceiving and dealing with that person that never occurred to you before.

Since the dominant hand is the hand of control, it is also the appropriate hand for writing out the voice of the more controlling person (the authority figure). It also follows that the non-dominant hand will express the part of you that feels out of control, overwhelmed, hurt, fearful, weak, "wimpy," rejected, punished, criticized. In other words, the *other hand* speaks for the victim of that dominating authority figure. In responding with your *other hand*, don't be polite and hold back any feelings. Being polite is supporting and keeping the lid on the unspoken, repressed part of you that needs to open up and speak its truth. When this kind of self-communication takes place, you then open up the possibility of healing the hurt parts of yourself. You may also improve your relationship with the other person. In doing this exercise for the first time, select a person whose behavior is currently a problem for you.

SPEAKING UP

1. Choose an authority figure in your life that you feel like talking to right now. Let this person write with your dominant hand in its typical authoritative and abusive "voice."
2. With your *other hand*, write or print your true feelings and reactions. Remember, don't hold back. Let it all out.
3. If there is more to express, continue dialoguing back and forth until both sides have had their say.

Afterward, note any new insights and feelings you have about the other person in your dialogue. If you still feel upset or unresolved about your relationship, continue doing dialogues. It may take time before things shift into new understanding. It's important to observe any changes in your actual dealings with this other person. One day you may be pleasantly surprised.

When I started writing my first book, *The Creative Journal*, I was hit by a paralyzing writer's block. For what seemed like days I sat motionless, staring at the blank white paper in my typewriter. Finally I realized that this was getting me exactly nowhere, so I grabbed my journal and did the following dialogue. I sassed back at the Inner Critic voice that was driving me crazy. It took me about ten minutes and it catapulted me through a seemingly impossible impasse. I ended up sailing through the writing of that book in half the amount of time I originally thought it would take. I started by writing out the voice of the Critic with my right or dominant hand. Then I responded with my left hand. Or, to be more accurate, my Creative Child answered back.

The Critic spoke first:

> CRITIC: You're no author. You can't write. Look at this stuff you've written. It's a mess, unclear, dry, garbled. You're wasting your time. No publisher is ever going to accept this.

Then the Creative Child answered back:

> *CHILD: I'm going to do it anyway in spite of you. You see, I am doing it. I haven't let you get me. You're the one who is wasting your time. Get lost, will you!*

You're no author. You can't write.
Look at this stuff you've written.
It's a mess, unclear, dry, garbled.
You're wasting your time.
No publisher is ever going to accept this.

I'M GOING TO DO
IT ANYWAY IN
SPITE OF YOU.
YOU SEE, I AM DOING
IT. I HAVEN'T
LET YOU GET ME
YOU'RE THE ONE
WHO IS WASTING
YOUR TIME.

GET LOST
WILL YOU.

Five years ago when I began working on this book, I was hit by another writer's block. It took the form of a hyperactive Critic (in my own mind) that scoffed at every sentence. I would write a few lines, crumple the page up and trash it. Another few lines, another crumpled wad of paper. Again and again, I hurled my written words into rejection. Frustrated beyond belief, I felt like the crazed writer played by Jack Nicholson in *The Shining*. In this film, Nicholson's writer's block manifests as page after page of the same sentence typed over and over again: "All work and no play makes Jack a dull boy." Nicholson's colossal block drives him crazy, to the point of attempting to murder his wife and child. Well, I didn't take it that far, but I did experience the lethal power of the Inner Critic. Make no mistake about it, that Inner Critic can be a killer.

Here is the dialogue in which I confronted the Inner Critic. My right hand started by simply observing the internal struggle I'd been having.

RIGHT HAND:

I'm feeling so stuck. I hear those voices saying: Waste of time. This isn't getting us anywhere. Stop this. Give up.

This cranky, pessimistic voice which writes in that cramped little handwriting is so negative. I see it so clearly.

This critical, judgemental,
pessimistic S.O.B. is
really awful-sounding
My little kid inside wants
to answer back.

Then the angry Inner Child answered back with the left hand. She asserted herself to the Critical voices in my head. She raged against the Inner Critic's put-downs.

LEFT HAND:

I've had enough of you,
no-no-no-no-no

LEFT HAND:

You get out, go talk to someone else, I am sick of being stuck. So shut up. I'm writing this book—I'm using both hands—I'm not going to let you get in my way. You can't

Control me. I know you're
trying but I have help.
I wish I could like you.
But you hurt me and try to
kill me. Why you scared or me?

Notice that the angry voice suddenly became vulnerable, as reflected in the small, shaky writing and the expression of hurt feelings. This often happens in fights between the right and left hand as well as between people in everyday life. When people risk showing the raw emotion of anger, they expose a part of themselves that is usually concealed. This kind of self-disclosure paves the way for deeper intimate sharing, such as feelings of tenderness or vulnerability.

The dialogue then continued with the Right Hand speaking for the Critic:

RIGHT HAND:

I want control. I want thinks to be the way I think they should be. I don't like the unexpected unless I can neatly fit it into my own plans and beliefs. That's all there is to it.

You are too unpredictable and spontaneous and uncontrollable. You make me very nervous. You do things that are unexplainable by me. You get emotional and I get completely disoriented. I don't know what to do with emotions & intuitions. They don't fit into my categories about what is knowable, prove-able. I just don't have the tools to deal with you. I know about logic & reason + planning + following rules + keeping to the letter of the law. If you start making changes then where will I be? Everything will be chaotic and unmanageable. We can't have that! We must have order. It's only right and correct!

Notice that the Critic started in a neat, "acceptable" style which became smaller and more cramped as the message became increasingly critical and up-tight. You can almost visualize the Critic character shriveling up in its own shell of intolerance and rigidity.

LEFT HAND:

Yeah but what about
fun + playing + laughing
If you didn't have the
unexpected how would
you have jokes. Jokes
are funny because
you don't expect what's
coming. It's not following
the "rules" of ordinary life.

RIGHT HAND:

Well, I guess a little of that is ok. But only within bounds. It can't get "out of hand"—we must keep some kind of law and order.

LEFT HAND:

What about love. Does law and order come before love?

RIGHT HAND:

Yes. Law & order comes first. that's the way I need it to be. Everything under my control. I'm God here. I run things. Don't forget it.

Notice that the right hand (Critic) continued getting smaller in its uptight scrawl. And it never gave up its ego mind-set. It ends the dialogue the way it started: stubborn and self-righteous, with small writing. With such a harsh taskmaster breathing down my neck, is it any wonder that I felt blocked, frustrated, incapable of continuing with my heart's desire: to write this book? But I continued working on the book. However, I gave that Critic a job to do: my taxes. Diverting it to a task it was ideally suited for, I persuaded it to leave my Inner Artist alone in peace.

This dialogue demonstrates the essence of a creative block. Part of us says, "Yes, I can." The other part says, "No, you can't." For every optimist, dreamer, or visionary living within us there is a critic, censor, or judge lurking about erecting an obstacle in our path. Whether our heart's desire is to learn to ski, to start our own business, to travel, or to attain inner peace, the game is the same: YES vs. NO.

Many people are blocked, but don't even know it. Their heart's desire is so deeply buried that it's almost dead. The symptoms are there, however, for these people feel chronically depressed, dull, and bored with life. I asked my left hand why this was so. Here is the answer I got:

LEFT HAND:

Any-
thing that's imprisoned
within us is using up an
equal amount of "creative"
energy to be it's jailer.
Do you understand what
I mean?

LEFT HAND:

Ask yourself: What am I afraid to express? And underneath that you will find creativity buried.

It takes a lot of energy to keep creativity buried. It's like plant life. You keep cutting it back + it keeps growing back. It persists.

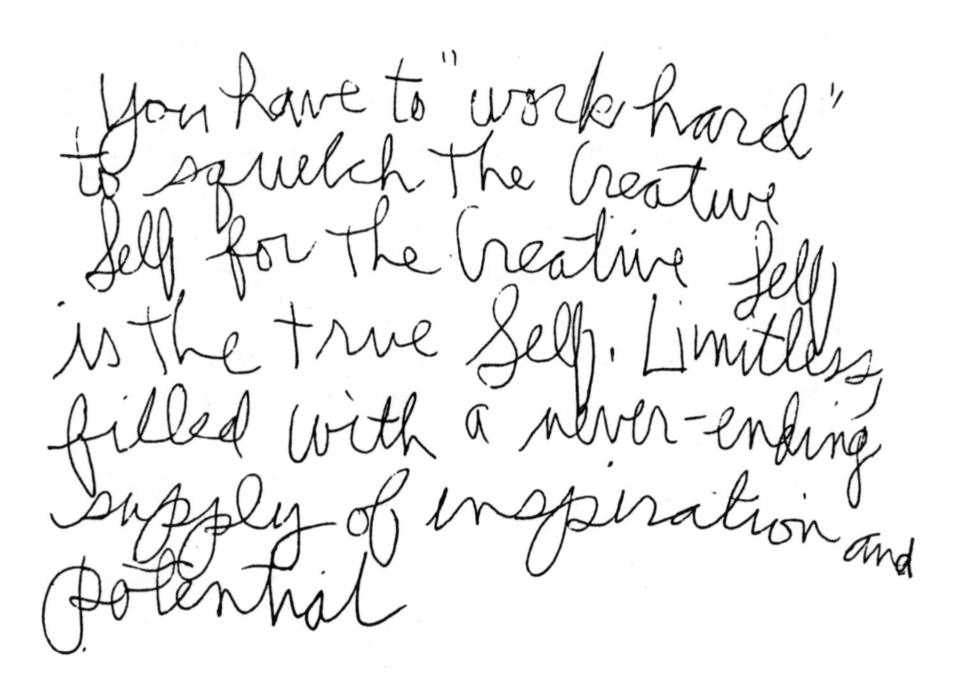

The upcoming exercise, Block Buster 1, is designed to help you get in touch with a particular "Heart's Desire": a secret wish to do or be something. This could be a dream from childhood, adolescent or adult years. You'll also have an opportunity to uncover conscious or unconscious aspects of yourself that say "NO" and prevent the fulfillment of your Heart's Desire. It may help to create two characters in your mind, one who represents your Heart's Desire and the other who speaks for your Block. Here are some examples:

HEART'S DESIRE	BLOCK
Artist	Perfectionist
Poet	Pessimist
Inventor	Critic
Explorer	Judge
Dreamer	Nag
Child	Pusher

Your Heart's Desire is still struggling to be born, so it speaks with your weaker, non-dominant hand. The Block is the controlling power right now—if that were not the case, you would have fulfilled your Heart's Desire already. So the Block writes with your controlling or dominant hand.

BLOCK BUSTER 1

1. Ask yourself: What is my Heart's Desire? What is the one thing I want to do, to be or to express that is currently being blocked?
2. Select or create two characters: One is your Heart's Desire and the other is your block.
3. Begin a written dialogue by letting your non-dominant hand express your Heart's Desire. Be as elaborate and detailed as you want.
4. Continue the dialogue by letting your dominant hand tell its story and why it blocks your desire.

This exercise will help you clarify your true Heart's Desire. Writing it out with your *other hand* makes it easier to sort out what *you really want*, not what others want for you. When you know what you *really* want and are willing to "go for it," a shift in power takes place. The Inner Critic eventually becomes impotent: an emperor with no clothes. The pseudo-rational arguments of the Critic are brought to light and revealed for what they are: negative self-fulfiling prophecies.

The following is a quick technique for dealing with writer's block. It opens up your creative inspiration by starting with your right brain (other hand), so that you can make some headway against that block.

BLOCK BUSTER 2

If you are having difficulty writing an assignment, a proposal, or some other project, try starting it with your non-dominant hand. When you've opened up the flow of words, when the writing is coming easily, go to the typewriter or computer and continue.

Elizabeth, an author and journal teacher, had a big breakthrough using this technique. Here is what happened, according to her account:

I had to write my autobiography for a graduate school program—put it off till the last minute, then just *couldn't* get started. I turned to my left hand and it said:

This is easy! I was there too—remember? Let's think together, 'cause I remember it all. I even remember our exact address back in Troy. What we liked doing best was to go up to the hills behind the little quarry and walk around and play. Come on—I'll give you the title and the first chapter heading—if you get stuck just come back to me. Ready? . . .

Then I went to the typewriter and wrote the following:

PLAYING IN THE HILLS
498 4th Street, Troy, New York: 1950

It was always best when the snow was gone, but just recently gone so that the ground was still wet underneath. I figured that was why it smelled so good, but your shoes didn't get muddy—because the snow had gone way, way underneath the ground and pushed up the grass.

There was a quarry there and a waterfall. I would climb the face of the rocks, right near the falls, to the top, and then walk along the stream, jumping across when something

> caught my interest. I knew that no one in the world had such wonderful adventures as I, no one was as brave, no one was as safe.
>
> The hills were just one block away from my street—the last street in a lingering city. We lived upstairs in a two-story house and Nana lived downstairs until she died on my father's birthday, which was three months before Danny was born. I liked Danny a lot right from the start. He was round and happy and had eyes like my father. Tom was my big brother and, after adoring him for the first few years of my life, I lost interest. My mother and father loved each other very much and I never heard them argue. I also never told them I spent my playtime living alone in the hills.
>
> My little friend, Theresa, never came with me because she was scared. But then, she was Polish and went to public school, so I didn't see her much anyway. We were Irish (except my mother was Austrian and my father was half Swedish) and we went to St. Joseph's School where each class had 58 children and each sister kept a paddle in her desk drawer. My father very carefully told me one day that I should respect the sisters and learn my lessons, but that no one, *no one*, would ever be allowed to hit me.
>
> So I would run to the hills without Theresa, without fear, because I thought my father meant I would always be safe . . . .

When I started seriously planning this book, I spent many days dialoguing back and forth between my right and left hand. I asked my left hand for some insight about itself. In its typically simple and clear language, it told me about *my* self.

LEFT HAND:

You have heard it before. It bears repeating. The truth will set you free.

The truth of which I speak is not a collection of material "facts." The truth is that you are the Self. You are guided by a deeper knowing and

you have it with you
at all times. The
right brain—the
left hand—these
are metaphors for
a kind of knowing
that goes beyond
fact, beyond
material world
logic, time +
space. As long
as you are in
the physical world

You need both kinds
of knowing -
logical and
intuitive. The logical
side only benefits
from the liberation
of the intuitive side,
for its burden is
lifted. Expecting
logic to do everything
is death. Expecting
intuition to do every-
thing is a denial of

a precious gift too,
your humanity consists
of both. Let the
two come together,
They were never
meant to be apart,
Let the left brain
understand what
the right brain knows.
Let the right hand
know what the left
hand is doing.

CHAPTER FOUR

Hand in Hand: Breaking Through

You need both kinds of knowing—logical and intuitive. Let the two come together. They were never meant to be apart.

—Lucia's left hand

It is the polarity and the integration of these two modes of consciousness, the complementary workings of the intellect and the intuitive, which underlies our highest achievement.

—Robert Ornstein
The Psychology of Consciousness

There is a current misconception that so-called *right-brain processing* is more creative than left-brain thinking. If creativity is defined only as inspiration, intuition, divergent thinking, then this may be so. However, if creativity is seen in the larger context of the *creative process*, this is not so. I define creativity as the ability to break through to new understanding or expression beyond what one has experienced before. This involves an expansion of awareness: a shift into a new way of seeing things. Creativity is also integrative, using "both kinds of knowing"—logical and intuitive—appropriately. At its highest, creativity allows us to have a vision and then apply our vision to everyday life. It is what Walt Disney called, "Imagineering."

Creativity is 5% inspiration, 95% perspiration.

—*Anonymous*

You can receive an inspiration or have a vision, but unless your logical, practical side is also active, the inspiration will die in the cemetery of ideas. Bright ideas are easy, application is not so easy. For example, having the vision to write a book and actually doing it are not the same thing. The idea is only the first step in a chain of events.

In his article, "Breakthrough into Insight," Joseph Chilton Pearce, author of *Magical Child* and *Crack in the Cosmic Egg,* presents a beautifully clear framework for the creative process. He calls it the *breakthrough process.* I believe they are the same.

> Breakthrough takes place in every discipline and every field of life. Studies of the phenomenon in science, art and religion describe five major steps in the breakthrough process.
>
> First is *commitment:* a person seizes a notion or idea, a desire for something currently unknown or unavailable. Then, at some point, that idea or possibility turns and seizes the one who had seized it. A once novel notion becomes a passionate, ultimate commitment.

My favorite example of this commitment phase comes from C. G. Jung. His commitment phase occurred in the wake of severing a close association with Freud. It was a time of great confusion and doubt for Jung, which threw him into a desperate search to find his own truth.

The decision to go on this quest took Jung into what Pearce refers to as the second phase: *service.* For six years Jung embraced what he called his "self experiment." His assistant and biographer, Aniela Jaffe, recounts that during this time Jung "went into a sort of meditation, often accompanied by strong emotion."

Jung painted and wrote about the symbols and images of his inner experiences in a journal called *The Red Book.* In masterly hand-lettered text and richly colored symbolic pictures from the unconscious, Jung plumbed the depths of his own psyche only to discover a universal, subterranean ocean. He called it the collective unconscious. His art work seems timeless. The medieval-looking calligraphy gives *The Red Book* the ancient quality of illuminated manuscripts. Archetypal images abound: mandalas, serpents, crosses, fire, and other motifs that appear in the art and architecture of ancient as well as modern civilizations. In his autobiography, *Memories, Dreams, and Reflections,* Jung wrote about this period:

> The years when I was pursuing my inner images were the most important in my life—in them everything essential was decided. It all began then; the later details are only supplements and clarifications of the material that burst forth from the unconscious, and at first swamped me. It was the *prima materia* for a lifetime's work.

According to Pearce, the third phase of the breakthrough process is a period of *gestation,* characterized by stuckness, dryness, disappointment, a dark night of the soul. It is at this point that many individuals fall into the obsessive-compulsive trap of forcing the "muse" or pushing for intellectual solutions by trying to "figure it out." The mind runs around in the old grooves of the known. This leads nowhere except deeper into the problem. At this point, the rational mind must surrender. It simply doesn't have the answers and must now renounce control. Einstein must have had this phase in mind when he said that "Imagination is greater than knowledge."

In his classic little volume on the creative process, *Letters to a Young Poet,* the great German poet, Rainer Maria Rilke, wrote with great feeling about the *gestation* period:

> . . . all progress must come from deep within and cannot be pressed or hurried by anything. *Everything* is gestation and then bringing forth. To let each impression and each germ of a feeling come to completion, wholly in itself, in the dark, in the inexpressible, the unconscious, beyond the reach of one's own intelligence, and await with deep humility and patience the birth-hour of a new clarity: that alone is living the artist's life: in understanding as in creating. There is here no measuring with time, no year matters, and ten years are nothing. Being an artist means, not reckoning and counting, but ripening

> like the tree which does not force its sap and stands confident in the storms of spring without the fear that after them may come no summer. It does come. But it comes only to the patient, who are there as though eternity lay before them, so unconcernedly still and wide. I learn it daily, learn it with pain to which I am grateful: *patience* is everything.

This lack of expectation or state of surrender is a clear field in which the mind stops struggling. This is fertile soil for the next phase: *breakthrough.*

Breakthrough happens in a flash of light illuminating the darkness. The history of science, art, and religion abounds with stories of sudden insight or blinding revelations. Pearce sites William Hamilton's discovery of the Quaternion Theory, a milestone in modern mathematics:

> . . . in a single instant as he idly crossed a bridge into Dublin while taking a walk to get away from his insurmountable problem. He had spent fifteen years of steady, dilligent, generally heartbreaking pursuit, before that insight-revelation flashed into view.

In other cases, *breakthrough* happens in dreams, as in the often-quoted case of Kekule's discovery of the benzene ring. He had exhausted himself trying to solve the problem, but in the relaxed dream state the answer presented itself in symbolic form: a serpent devouring its own tale, the archetypal image of the "ouroborus." Interestingly, this same image appears in Jung's work in a psychological context. For him the ouroborus symbolized the paradox of life and death.

According to Pearce, the fifth and final stage of the breakthrough process is the result of the previous four (commitment, service, gestation, and breakthrough). It is *translation* or application into useful form. It cuts across all areas of activity and can include everything from creating a new recipe to living out a spiritual revelation. Pearce points out that the "nature of the breakthrough is determined by the nature of the search, and by the depth of passionate commitment given it."

After his moment's insight, Hamilton spent fifteen years in the practical translation of his mathematical theory. It took Jung a lifetime to bring forth the discoveries and insights gained during his "self experiment." In his autobiography he wrote, "It has taken me virtually forty-five years to distill within the vessel of my scientific work the things I experienced and wrote down at the time. . . My works are a more or less successful endeavor to incorporate this incandescent matter into the contemporary picture of the world."

Since I began teaching and lecturing on the subject of writing with the *other hand,* I have seen many breakthroughs. Most of my workshop participants and private clients chose to write with their *other hand.* However, I have met some individuals who were forced by circumstances to write with their non-dominant hand. A broken arm or wrist, a stroke, or some other sudden injury or illness led to a temporary or permanent switch to the *other hand.* Many of these individuals experienced deep inner changes, opened undeveloped dimensions of their personalities, and uncovered buried talents.

Brad is a case in point. An attractive and energetic young man, Brad was in his early twenties when I interviewed him. He told me how he had discovered a whole new world because of an accident which forced him to write with the *other hand.* Here is Brad's story:

> As a young child I wrote stories and had a large imaginary world to play in. My neighborhood appeared to be a boundless garden of adventure, mystery, danger, and fun. My travels turned wide curves that flowed back to their origin without effort or need to remember details. My days flowed together and I was very happy.
>
> I had an obsession for games and a terrible fear of losing or being rejected. As a young boy I ran away from my first baseball game crying because I had run the wrong direction around the bases. At an early age I was made to realize that if I wanted to play men's games I had to learn the rules and pay attention to detail. I saw that a man's world is very critical. Judgments are made with large consideration to the end goal,

and the means are carefully restricted to the straightest line toward that goal.

So I set out to learn the rules, and I learned them better than anyone else, to the point of being able to tell my coaches when they had made mistakes before they recognized them. I learned to direct all my anger and desires toward the goal: winning.

I lost sight of my fluid, youthful world as I grew up and became more and more rigid in body and spirit. I tried to take on the outer appearances and inflexible standard of a winner. I was quarterback and team captain at school, a leader on the field, a sacrificer of my body. I could throw a footbal 75 yards at age 15. I pitched on the baseball team and developed a keen jump shot and hook in basketball. My right arm spent long days reaching, throwing, and extending. I did little reading but did well in school, especially in math and sciences. My language skills were poor. I always worked hardest in this area and received my worst grades in English and foreign languages. At 15 I had many male friends in high school and almost no female friends. In those days I preferred a good dirt-ball game to a date.

It is still very vivid in my memory, the day I fell to the floor on the basketball court of my high school with a pain so strong in my right shoulder and arm that somehow I knew instantly my dreams were shattered. I knew I would never play professional football as I so fervently desired. In fact, later I found out that I would never be able to throw any kind of ball again.

A week later I sat at my final examination in English with a dislocated right arm. I was very angry because the teacher was forcing me to write my essay with my left hand. My right arm was tightly bound to my body and totally immobile. I had been confident I would get off without writing any essay that day, which would have been fine with me. Soon I found out that if I didn't write one I could fail the class. I spent almost three hours completely absorbed in my new and arduous task. I found myself using all the pent-up anger and frustration as fuel to write a very long, barely legible and somewhat sarcastic essay. By the time I turned my paper in I had forgotten how enraged I had been or that so much time had passed. Taking charge of my emotions had required great effort.

Afterwards I felt vulnerable, exhausted, and close to tears. Yet I wouldn't dare let these feelings out. I couldn't ride my bike so I walked home three miles. My shoes came untied many times but I got great satisfaction out of tying them with my left hand. At home I became completely fanatical about keeping my life's routines as normal as possible with the use of only my left arm. I cooked, wrote papers, made telephone calls, drove a car, and performed personal hygiene with my left hand. Every little detail became intensified, important, difficult, and exciting. Everything in my life became a challenge which was solely designed to teach me a lesson: that I could do something which I had thought I couldn't do. This in turn gave me new self-confidence and opened a previously unknown world to me.

I received a "C" grade on my English essay. I hadn't given enough, the teacher seemed to be saying, but that essay was the beginning of a major transformation in my life. I couldn't use my right arm for six weeks, and just after getting the cast off I injured it again. During this time I became totally focused on reading and writing. The more I read, the more my child-like curiosity surfaced. My visual imagination overflowed in long and insightful reports, essays and poetry. My grades in English went from "C" to "A".

As my inner life expanded, so did my friends and surroundings. During the recuperation I was separated from my jock friends who, it turned out, were not very good friends after all. So I had to create new friendships, most of them with women. I found I could talk to them more easily about my new feelings. And I fell in love for the first time.

> Along with these changes, I also wanted to move out of the city. I really felt the need to get in touch with the natural rhythms and patterns of life, with my body and spirit. So I went to live in the woods until I entered college to study another physical discipline: dance.

Brad opened up to his own creativity and entered the arts world when he turned a catastrophe into a golden opportunity. He went on to become a performing dancer and instructor of Contact Improvisation, a new movement form. His unique style combines fluidity and strength: power that expresses a balance he has attained between the active and receptive aspects of his personality. Brad attributes the beginning of this major life change to the day he dislocated his arm and was forced to use his *other hand.*

Words have continued to be an important outlet for Brad, who later studied acting. As he told me: "When I started focusing on acting, I found myself writing in mirror images with my left hand. It was spontaneous and completely unexpected. I feel it has stretched my awareness in exciting ways."

The "mirror writing" that Brad refers to is simply the act of writing backward. It is a mirror image of "normal" writing and is legible when reflected in a mirror. Otherwise it is difficult to decipher. Leonardo da Vinci wrote entire notebooks in this way. The theory is that he wanted to keep his ideas a secret, so he recorded them in an unreadable form. But I wonder? Perhaps Leonardo's *other hand* wrote those notebooks, or maybe he chose to write backwards in order to "see things from a different perspective." Regardless of his reasons, this practice of writing backward may have contributed to his unique way of looking at the world. Incidentally, I've read that Leonardo was left-handed, so his *other hand* would have been his right hand.

I've discussed my questions about Leonardo's motives for mirror writing with movement specialist Grant Ramey. I was studying movement with Grant when I first started writing this book, but it wasn't until several years later that I learned he was a mirror writer. As a young child, he was right-handed, but at ten or twelve years of age he started asking questions about his hands. They looked alike, why couldn't they do the same things? In sports, he started experimenting with using both his right and left hand. He used his left hand for free throws and lay-up shots in basketball, for serving and hitting in volleyball, and holding the paddle in ping-pong. Grant even tried favoring his weaker foot in soccer, surfing, and skateboarding. He also became ambidextrous in carpentry.

After college, Grant went to Liberia, West Africa, on a Peace Corps assignment. Living for twenty-one months in a small village with nothing much to do for entertainment, he started keeping a journal. Although he had been to college, Grant reports that he truly became literate while writing his African journals. Prior to that, reading and writing had always been duties rather than sources of personal satisfaction. He studied the roots of words and developed a fascination for the Thesaurus.

Grant's interest in writing eventually led to his discovery of writing with the *other hand*. By this time he was in his late twenties and had written exclusively with his right hand. He now decided to extend his self-taught ambidexterity to writing. When he did this, it came out backward in mirror printing that looked child-like. He remembers having felt a tickling sensation in his brain. As he put it: "I knew that new things were happening." He continued doing mirror printing and then mirror writing in longhand. Within a year he was doing all of his journal entries in mirror writing. He also carried on a mirror-writing correspondence with someone who also wrote in this manner. To this day, Grant writes personal notes, telephone messages, and "To Do" lists backward with his left hand.

A graphologist once analyzed Grant's right-hand normal writing and his left-hand mirror writing and observed that both hands had the same personality traits. This is an interesting contrast to the thousands of samples I've seen of normal left-to-right handwriting done with both hands. As I'll discuss later, the two hands almost always differ in the style and characteristics of their writing.

Grant was aware of Leonardo da Vinci's mirror-written notebooks. We discussed my theory that Leonardo might have done the mirror writing with his non-dominant hand. Might he have known that "new things were happening" when he wrote this way? Was he using this technique in order to reach for harmony and inner vision not possible through standard writing? As a movement specialist, Grant saw a connection between mirror writing and Leonardo's passionate interest in symmetry and the human form in art and in science.

Grant's own lifelong fascination with mirroring and balance in the human body led him away from sports and into the discovery of a new system of body movement which he calls, Embodiment. This method emphasizes awareness of how all parts of the body interrelate as a whole. Grant's goal is "giving bodily form to the Divine Self through conscious and natural movement."

Mirror writing teaches concentration. It becomes a form of meditation forcing you to stay in the moment. You have to slow down and become one-pointed on what you are doing. It requires that you focus your mind so that it doesn't wander off in a myriad of unrelated and inconsequential thoughts. Also we don't know how to picture mirror writing in our minds very well, if at all, so we have to stay with the actual kinesthetic sense of moving our hand across the page and forming the letters one at a time.

Why not try mirror writing? It's a wonderful way to break old patterns and shift perception. Yes, it will probably feel awkward and look strange. It may be totally unreadable unless you hold it up to a mirror. It may also shake you out of your old ways and into a new perspective. You may get a glimmer of what Leonardo experienced when he did mirror writing.

MIRROR WRITING

1. Using your *other hand*, print or write your name backward. Then in the same mirror writing describe, in a sentence or two, how it feels to write backward.
2. Now, read what you wrote. If you have a mirror handy, hold your paper up to it and read what you wrote by looking at the mirror's reflection.

As we have seen from Brad's and Grant's stories, ambidexterity (by necessity or by choice) can have an expansive influence on one's life. The following exercise is intended to open you up to the possibility of using both hands to do tasks you ordinarily do with one hand. Observe yourself as you do the exercise. Be aware of how you feel physically and emotionally. Since you are probably less coordinated with your *other hand*, the tasks will probably go slower than usual. Allow more time to do the activities. One of the purposes of doing things with your *other hand* is to encourage you to stay in the moment and be attentive to your movements. This can have a very relaxing effect, if you will take it easy and not try to hurry or pressure yourself to perform as well as you do with your dominant hand.

AMBIDEXTERITY

Try switching hands for some of the daily activities listed below:

1. Brushing your teeth
2. Combing or brushing your hair
3. Opening and closing doors
4. Getting dressed and undressed
5. Eating and drinking
6. Picking objects up and putting them down

Another person who blossomed when she discovered her non-dominant hand is Mona Brookes, a drawing teacher who helps people of all ages find the hidden Artist within. Children and adults come to her with the common complaint, "I can't draw." At the end of their first art lesson each person walks out with amazement and pride saying, "I can't believe I drew this picture." She has written a book about her Monart Method entitled, *Drawing with Children*.

When I met Mona in 1981, I gave her a copy of my first book, *The Creative Journal: The Art of Finding Yourself*. In her first right/left-hand dialogue, she asked a question and got a very wise answer from her non-dominant left hand. Although the handwriting was shaky, the message was powerful and clear.

Lefthanded

Thank you Lucia:
I ask for guidance in following
a divine pathway. Please help
me in finding the True and
beautiful answers to
my spiritual evolvement.

answer #1

Don't ever forget the
children. Relate!
Love!

A few days later, Mona alternated writing with both hands. She observed that each hand had its own distinct style of handwriting. This has been the case with all of the thousands of students and clients I've observed. For instance, if the dominant handwriting slants in one direction, the non-dominant handwriting usually slants in the opposite direction. Mona's right and left handwriting demonstrates this clearly, as shown in the following pages.

RIGHT HAND:

Total Eclipse of The Moon
Mona

Healing
Air Thru The Body
Become Negative Space
Mona is finding the left side
of her body and the right
side of her mind. There is no
reason I can't repair the left
hand to do anything I want it to.
Thank you again Lucia.

I promise the moon I would

would stop trying to control
everything and let Universal
Mind unfold a devine plan. But
truth, please help me sort out
the shaft from the wheat.

Help me make Love and caring
my guiding Light.

In another journal entry, Mona expressed a profound insight with the simplicity and clarity that is typical of writing done with the *other hand.* Notice how the handwriting is becoming stronger and more legible than her first attempts. One day while writing with her left hand,

Mona changed the angle of the paper to approximate the angle it occupies when she writes with her right hand. At that moment, her left handwriting became smaller and more controlled. Notice the change in size mid-way through the paragraph.

Compitition is a killer. School systems instill tremendous competition. I want a school where there is no competition and there is room for everyone to be a winner and be the wonderful person they already are.

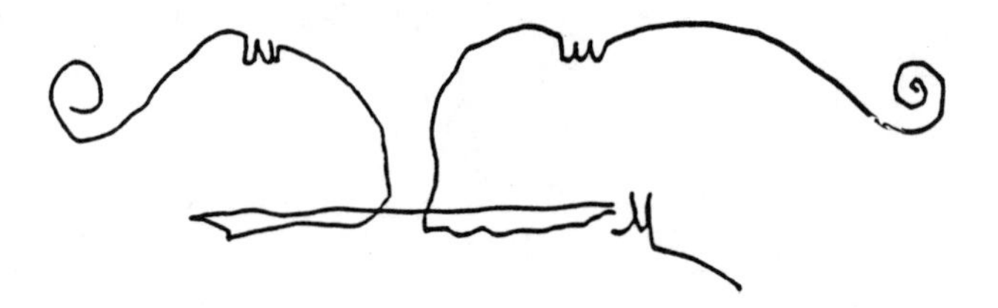

Dear Lucia:

I am writing this with my lefthand. Today, I have had a breakthru with the small motor co-ordination. It makes it possible to write much smaller.

Love,
Mona

Here is what she said about her experience:

> When I changed the angle of the paper so that my arm and hand were in the same relationship to the paper as they are when I write with my right hand, something happened. At that moment my left hand gained small motor control and coordination and was able to write smaller and more legibly. Once I analyzed how my right hand went about writing, its movement pattern and the direction of the paper, I was able to write with my left hand in a flash! Yes, I could write with my left hand although I never thought I could. And in that moment I understood how my method of teaching drawing works. It's simply a question of physically experiencing one's ability to do it and then dropping the old belief that says, "I can't do this. I don't know how. I'm not capable of it." Once you actually do it, these arguments lose their power. And that's when the creative block disintegrates. I suddenly realized that this is the secret to my drawing method—a new way of seeing.

Creative breakthroughs are experiential. They don't come from intellectual analysis. In other words, it's simply a matter of finding the "key" to unlock the door of percetion. A new way of seeing things can change everything in an instant. And creative breakthrough comes from Inner Wisdom, which I define as *intuitive knowing from within.* It is not learned, influenced, or perceived from outside our own experience. It unfolds from inside out.

Another observation of Mona's was that she had to be willing to let her *other hand* have its own style of handwriting, its own personality, one that was natural and consistent but not at all like the writing of her dominant hand.

Mona was able to accept her left-hand expression for what it was: different. She didn't try to force it to write in the same style as her right hand. She saw it had uniqueness and validity in its own right. She treated the individual expression of her own left hand with the same respect and support she shows her art students.

Mona was so impressed with the psychological and perceptual awareness she gained from writing with her *other hand* that she incorporated this technique into her Monart lessons. She recommended that her new students do right/left hand dialogues with their creative blocks about drawing. She also suggested that they ask their non-dominant hand to write answers to the queston, "Why am I afraid to draw?" She reported good results.

Then Mona cultivated ambidexterity for other activities in her life. For instance, she switched over and brushed her teeth every day with her left hand. She noticed changes in her Tai Chi and did other body movements in perfect symmetry while watching herself in the mirror. Then she started drawing with her left hand and noticed a looseness and feeling of contentment. Three of her drawings are shown here.

The floral piece was drawn with her right (dominant hand), the drawing of feet was drawn with her left hand, and the drawing of a person was done with her left hand.

Mona experienced a chain reaction of creative breakthroughs in all areas of her life following her work with the non-dominant hand. What is so extraordinary about Mona's experience is the *speed* with which her blocks vanished. Like the domino effect, she watched one obstacle after another tumble before her eyes. This is not to say that right/left hand writing was solely responsible for the changes in Mona's life. However, it was a big catalyst for these changes.

One of Mona's most immobilizing blocks was a "travel phobia." She had just turned forty-five but had never traveled because she was afraid of getting lost, missing planes, or entering new environments. Shortly after she started doing left-hand writing and drawing she worked up the courage to take a car trip from Los Angeles to Santa Fe, New Mexico, with a friend. There were many complications on this trip serving to test Mona's "travel phobia." However, in the end, she had a wonderful time. "It was the first vacation I ever enjoyed," she recalled with a big smile. She has since become a confirmed traveler.

RIGHT-HANDED DRAWING

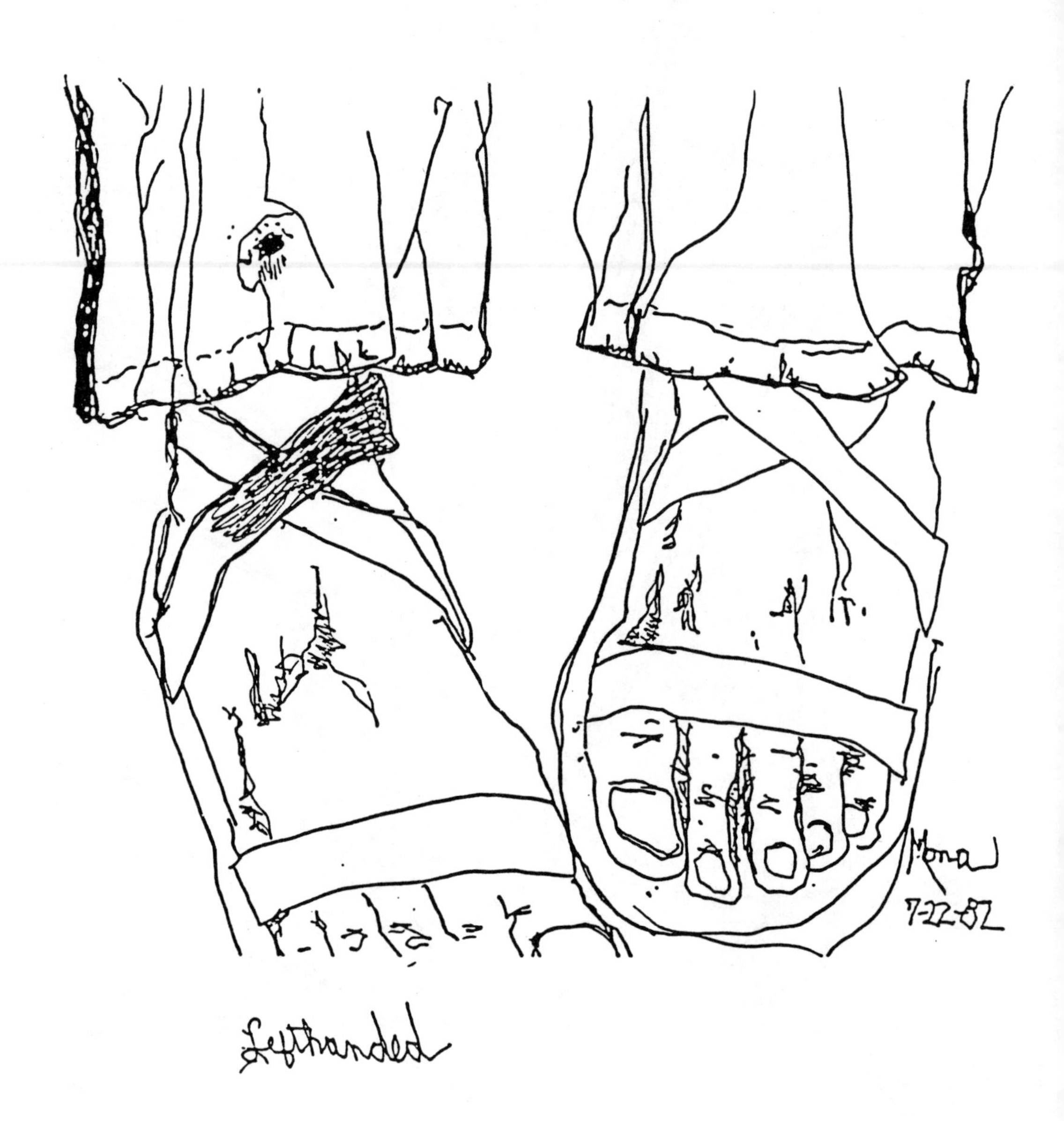
Mona
7-22-82
Lefthanded

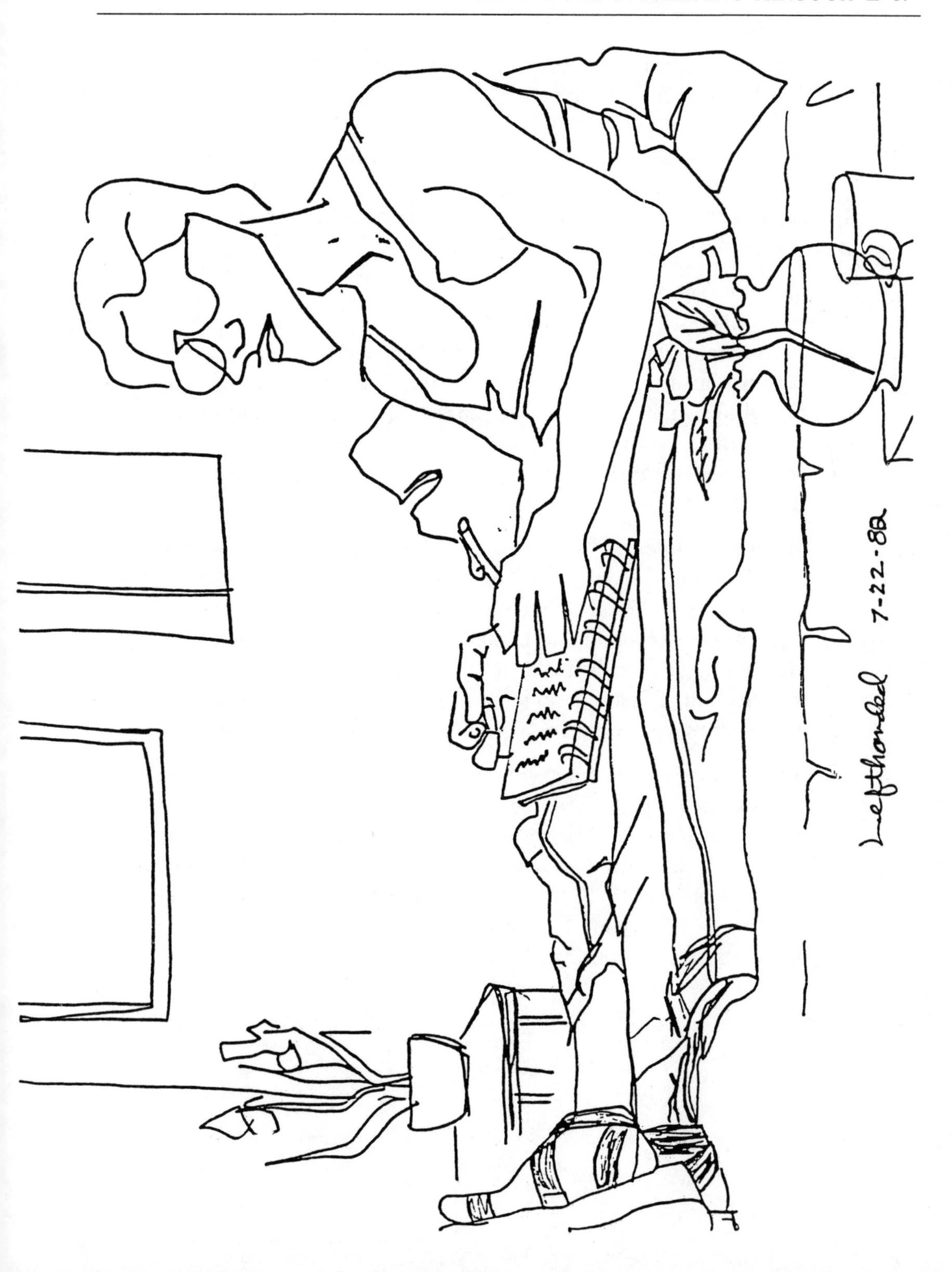
Lefthanded 7-22-82

One of the rewards of removing blocks is that it builds self-confidence. The breakthrough of the travel experience gave Mona the confidence to overcome other obstacles. She gained faith in her ability to play the piano. She accelerated the dance studies which she had recently embarked upon. At first she was extremely self-conscious and shy about dancing in front of others. She now dances with professionals and has appeared in a dance-movement video.

Mona also took on new challenges in business. Before founding her own art school, Mona had been a public servant. "I never saw myself as a businesswoman," she said. "I never dreamed that I was capable of going into business for myself. But after doing all these other things I thought I couldn't do, I started expanding my classes and trained many more instructors in my method." She also developed programs in public schools and in two years' time expanded from 350 to over 5,000 students.

Mona experimented with new ways of presenting her Monart exercises, drawing the design upside down as well as right to left and bottom to top. She also encouraged ambidextrous behavior in her students. It all added up to breaking old patterns, getting unstuck, pulling out of ruts. That's the key to the creative process. As Mona recommends, "Put yourself in an uncomfortable position. Feel awkward and observe how you relate to discomfort. Then push through it."

By now you can see that there are many, many ways to write which you probably never considered before. If you've done the earlier exercises, you've written with your non-dominant hand, you've had a dialogue between both hands, you've written backward in mirror fashion. So, it's time to write with both hands at the same time. Now you are probably thinking that I've gone too far. Please suspend your judgment for a few moments and try your hands at this new technique.

BOTH HANDS NOW

Materials: two felt pens, unlined paper.

1. With a pen in each hand, simultaneously doodle or draw any image that comes to mind. Draw the same image with both hands as shown in the illustration below.
2. Using both hands at the same time, write: "Now is the time for my heart's desire to come true."

Here is an example of one of Mona's doodle/writings done with two hands simultaneously.

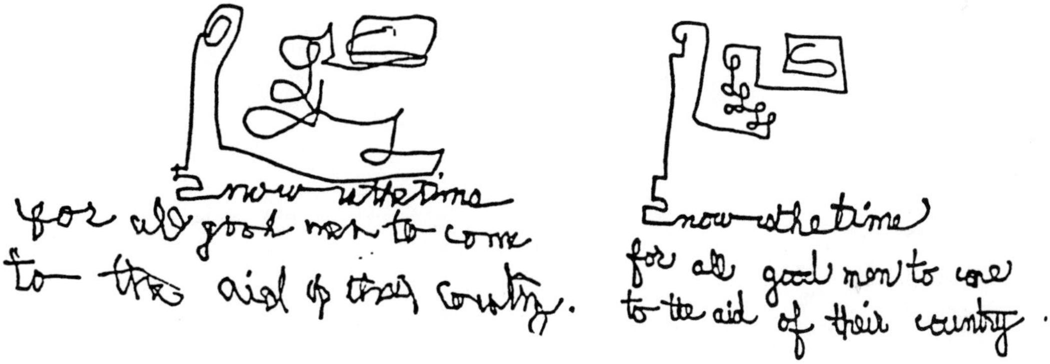

Many of my clients and students have reported that rapid life changes follow after starting to write and draw with the *other hand.* The same phenomenon applies in each case: the mind says, "I think I can't do this." The person *does* the action and thereby disproves the old belief. Once the action is done the mind says, "Now I *can* do this. If I can do this, what else can I do that I thought I couldn't do?" At this point, self-confidence takes a quantum leap, leaving one standing at the doorway to the next challenge and breakthrough.

CHAPTER FIVE

Finding the Artist Within

We will now apply both practical techniques and psychological tools to freeing the Artist Within. You may discover a natural talent for drawing hidden in your *other hand.* Why do I say this? We know from scientific research that, in most cases, the brain's right hemisphere controls the non-writing hand. And the right brain has its own set of abilities: visual/spatial perception, pattern and face recognition, the ability to synthesize and process information simultaneously (as in an all-at-once glance). These are precisely the abilities one needs in order to draw pictures. Betty Edwards points out these special capabilities of the right hemisphere in her book, *Drawing on the Right Side of the Brain.*

> One of the marvelous capabilities of the right brain is imaging: seeing an imaginary picture with your mind's eye. The brain is able to conjure an image and then "look" at it, "seeing" it as if it is "really there." The terms of this ability, visualizing and imaging, are used almost interchangeably . . . Both visualizing and imaging are important components of the skill of drawing. To draw something, an artist looks at the object or person, takes a mental picture, holds the image in memory, then looks down at the paper to draw. Another look, another held image, further drawing, and so on.

Before we turn to drawing, however, we must first be aware of the *psychological forces* that keep the Artist Within locked in the closet. Once we have recognized that there is an Artist Within, then we have a choice of whether or not to express it. But if we don't even know it's there, we'll never go looking for it.

Prior to becoming an Art Therapist, I worked in the field of Art Education. My first students were adults in a drawing and mixed media class, then pre-school and elementary-age children, and then teachers. This is what I discovered. Almost without exception, the pre-school age children embraced arts activities with eagerness and a sense of adventure. Their work had *life* in it. The school-age children exhibited embarrassment and self-criticism about their art. The older they were, the more self-conscious they were. By adolescence, a strong Inner Critic was busy at work. Enthusiasm for art was nearly extinguished. By adulthood, almost everyone was convinced they couldn't draw. Most of my work was remedial, helping revive the natural but lost ability which, I believe, is a universal human trait.

Over the years, I have asked hundreds of students the question: "Will the people who think they *can't* draw please raise their hands?" I've always gotten the same response: 75% to 85% raise their hands immediately. In an attempt to demonstrate that these beliefs are learned, I then ask the self-styled "non-artists" to tell me about their experiences with art. I've always heard the same set of answers:

> My first-grade teacher said I didn't have any talent.
>
> My mother threw my pictures in the trash.
>
> My father told me I was wasting time when I drew pictures.
>
> My classmates laughed at my art work in school.
>
> My sister was such a good artist, I just gave up because my art was so pathetic by comparison.
>
> My brother told me my art was for girls and sissies, and I should be out playing football with the boys.

If you think you can't draw, ask yourself the question: Who said so? Was it someone from your childhood? Was it you? Did you compare yourself to Rembrandt and conclude you had no talent? Examine your own beliefs about the Artist Within.

It is obvious to me that *we are all artists* until some are brain-washed into thinking otherwise. Very few escape. *Judgment, competition, and ridicule are the enemies of artistic ability. But that ability can be revived at any age in an atmosphere of support, safety, and love.* Love is the key. The great artist, Marc Chagall (known for his child-like paintings), puts it beautifully:

> Despite the trouble of our world, I have kept the love of the inner life in which I was raised and man's hope in love. In our life there is a single color, as on an artist's palette, which provides the meaning of life and art. It is the color of love. I see in this color of love all the qualities permitting accomplishment in all fields. I have often used the word chemistry in art. This chemistry can also exist in life itself. I often wonder why in this grandiose nature, man sometimes seems so cruel. I ask myself how that can be when alongside are the Mozarts, Beethovens, Shakespeares, Giotos, Rembrandts, and so many others, as well as all the humble and honest workers who built cathedrals, monuments, and works of art, and those who have invented all the things that improve and facilitate our lives. Is it possible that with all the new means of mastery, man is incapable of mastering himself? That to me is something inadmissable. One must not search outside nature but within oneself, where the keys to harmony and happiness lie. They are in our own hands. Everything I have tried to do is a weak response to this challenge. The art I have practiced since my childhood has taught me that man is capable of love and that love can save him. That, to me, is the true color, the true substance of art. It is as natural as a tree or a stone. All my works, here and there, are reflections of all I have seen, as in a sky, and felt every day in my soul. I have tried to keep all that in my heart.

Now you might be wondering: What is the connection between drawing and writing, other than the fact that they're both done with the hands? How does the *other hand* hand figure into drawing? There is a big connection.

The "I can't draw" notion is simply a belief, like thinking you can't write with your *other hand.* If you've done the earlier exercises in this book, you've discovered that you *can* write with your *other hand.* And when you do, you gain access to other parts of yourself.

The "I can't draw" notion leads to a shutdown of the Artist Within. If you *think* you can't draw, if you think you'll make mistakes and look foolish, you won't even attempt it. Your Inner Critic has won out. And with no exercise, artistic ability atrophies. It's a vicious circle, and in the end every part of your personality loses.

So now let's break out of that false belief. Let's start with some "loosening-up" exercises to activate both hands and both sides of your brain. These activities are intended to encourage a sense of playfulness and exploration that are common to both children, artists, and innovators in all fields.

Many people report that they use two-handed drawing exercises as a stress reduction technique. It clears the mind, calms the nerves, relaxes and opens up a child-like part of the self that longs to come out and play. Next time you feel frazzled and upset, try one or more of these drawing activities using both hands. It just might do wonders.

LOOK MA, BOTH HANDS

1. Take a pen in each hand and draw a symmetrical design using both hands at the same time. You will be creating a design in which each hand's drawing is a mirror image of the other.

LOOK MA, BOTH HANDS II

2. With a pen in each hand draw an identical doodle with both hands at the same time. Create your own abstract design and draw them side by side as shown in the illustration below.

LOOK MA, BOTH HANDS III

3. Continue drawing simultaneously with a pen in each hand. This time let each hand draw its own spontaneous image. Let each one do its own unique dance.

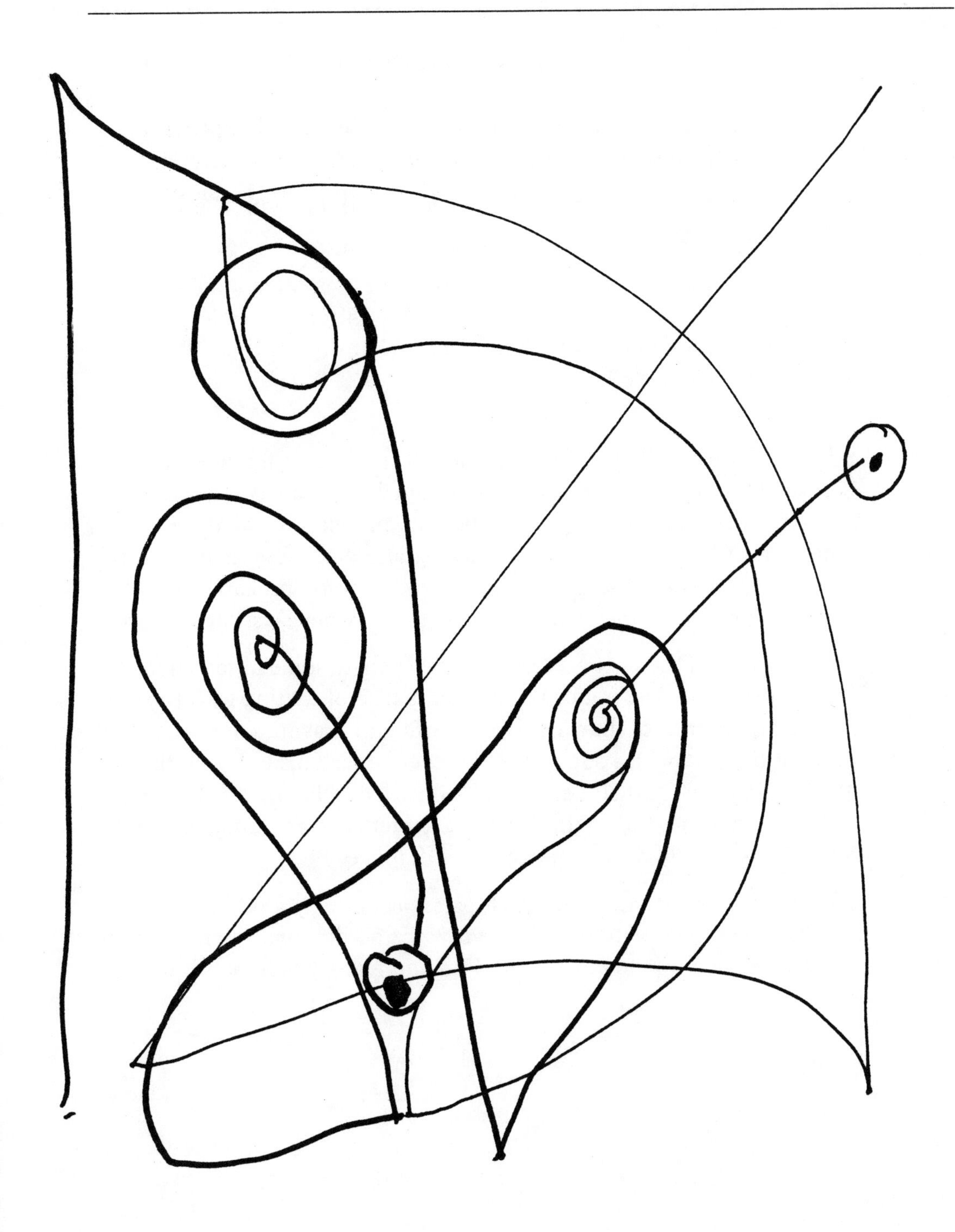

DOODLE HAND JIVE

1. Doodle or scribble with your dominant hand expressing whatever you feel right now.
2. Now switch hands and doodle or scribble with the non-dominant hand.

How did it feel to doodle with your dominant and non-dominant hands? Did you notice any difference in feeling? In coordination? In final product? What do you think about the two doodles?

Now that the Child in you has come out to play, we'll invite the Artist in you to draw an object in your environment. If you classify yourself as a non-artist, this task may seem insurmountable. You may be getting nervous at the very thought of drawing an object. You may be anticipating embarrassment and failure just the way you probably did before *writing* with your *other hand.* But you just may have a surprise in store.

Before you do the next exercise, I'd like to share some observations and some drawings. I've noticed that what is true of writing with the *other hand* is also true of drawing. Dominant-hand drawings are usually different from drawings done with the *other hand.* This has been the case for experienced "artists" as well as "non-artists." Each hand has its own style. Sometimes the contrast is great, sometimes it is subtle. But so far, there has usually been a noticeable difference.

In the drawings that follow, each pair was done by a different person. In each set, one picture was drawn with the dominant hand and one was produced by the *other hand.* Can you guess which one is which?

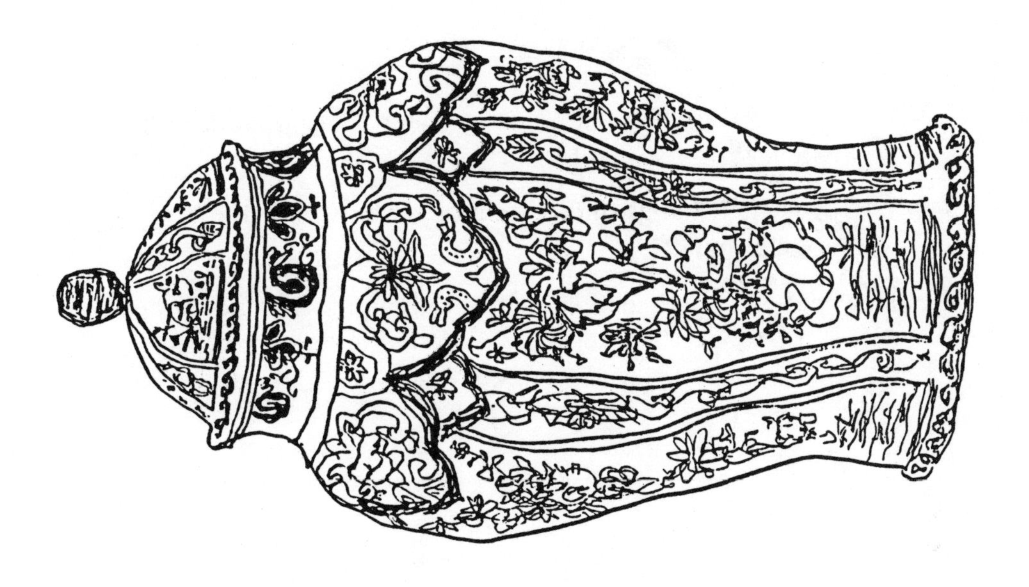

GINGER JAR

WOMAN

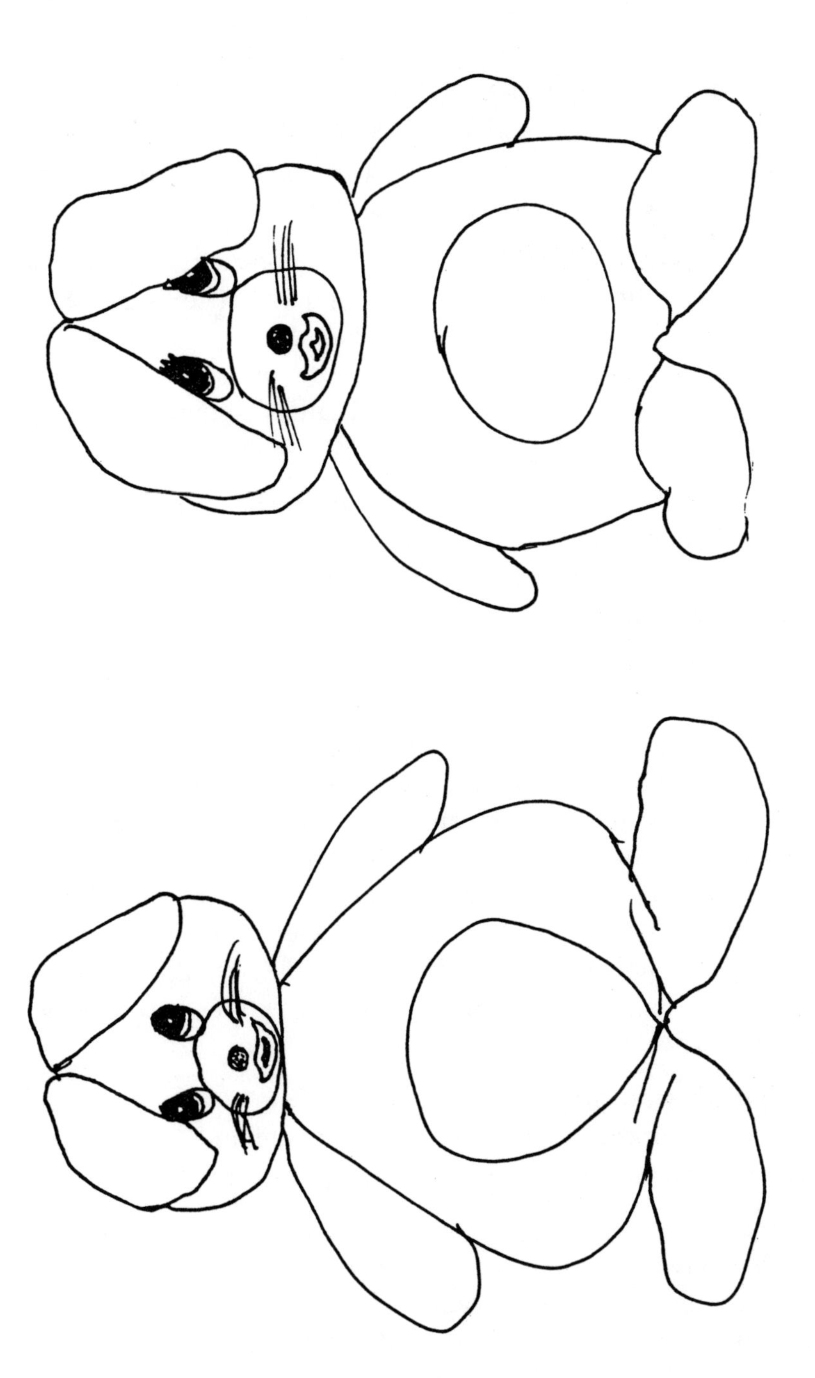

BUNNY

The drawings of the Ginger Jar are by me: a right-handed, trained professional artist. The picture on the left was drawn with the right (dominant) hand, the one on the right was done with the left (non-dominant) hand. The left-handed drawing is a more "realistic" representation of the subject in terms of contours, proportion, and decorative detail.

The drawings of a Woman were done by a non-artist. The one on the left was done with the left (non-dominant) hand. The face on the right was drawn with the right (dominant) hand. Like the Ginger Jar, the drawing by the non-dominant hand shows more sensitivity and is the rendering of a real woman's face rather than a two-dimensional stylized cartoon.

The Bunny was drawn by a young woman who has drawn all her life using her dominant hand only. The drawing on the left (done with the non-dominant hand) is more visually accurate than the drawing done with her dominant hand.

Many "non-artists" have found that when they draw the same subject, first with one hand and then the other, it is the non-dominant hand which reproduces visual designs, patterns, and form with much greater accuracy. In still lifes drawn with the non-dominant hand, the spatial relationships and proportions tend to be more accurate, compositions more balanced, and there is more depth and attention to detail. This always comes as a big surprise because people begin this exercise saying, "I can't draw with my dominant hand, how do you expect me to draw with my non-dominant hand?" Yet, when they try it, they often discover hidden ability, sophistication, and a level of esthetics far beyond what they expected.

Many people who thought they couldn't draw at all found that they *could* draw when they used their non-dominant hand. Contrary to their expectations, it was the "awkward" hand that was the artist.

The superior artistic ability of the non-dominant hand might be attributable to two factors. First, if the individual's non-dominant hand is being controlled by the right brain (which specializes in visual/spatial perception), then it makes sense that the non-dominant hand would draw better. Drawing is a visual/spatial activity.

Just as important is the fact that the non-dominant hand draws more slowly because it has less practice and training. In drawing from life, this is a definite advantage. It can force the person to slow down and really look at the subject instead of drawing quickly what he or she "thought" the eye saw. When I taught life drawing, the greatest challenge was getting the student to really *see* the subject, to *feel* the spaces and contours of that particular flower or basket, instead of drawing preconceived notions of how a flower or basket "should" look or has looked in the past.

Experienced artists (people trained in art or working as professionals) also find that the right hand draws differently from the left. A drawing done with the *other hand* is less controlled, looser, and often has an entirely different style. It is sometimes more humorous and captures the essence of the image rather than being a mere photographic representation. I've spoken to a number of professional artists who said they draw with their non-dominant hand in order to warm up and get their creative juices flowing. When these artists switch to their dominant hand, their work improves. This is essentially the same strategy Elizabeth used when she *wrote* with her *other hand* in order to break a writer's block.

The next two still lifes were done by a woman attending a drawing workshop. She had no previous training in art. The first drawing was done with her dominant right hand. The second drawing, done with her *other hand,* is more visually true to the subject. The perspective, proportions, and contours are more representational, and the composition is better than the drawing done with her dominant hand.

DOMINANT (RIGHT) HAND

NON-DOMINANT (LEFT) HAND

Now it's time for you to draw. This time you will select a simple object in your environment. Find something you really enjoy looking at. And just remember, no one is going to see these drawings but you. No one else is going to judge them. Recall also, that many people who thought they couldn't draw at all found they could draw with their non-dominant hand.

So take it easy, relax and do the next exercise. You may have a treat in store.

DRAWING WITH THE OTHER HAND

1. Choose a simple object. Look at it carefully and draw a picture of the object with your dominant hand.
2. Draw a picture of the object again, using your *other hand* this time.

How did it feel to draw with your dominant hand? With your non-dominant hand? Which drawing was easier to do? Compare your pictures. Do you notice differences between them. Do you like one better than the other? If so, why?

Experiment by drawing another object using your non-dominant hand for the first drawing and your dominant hand for the second. See what kind of results you get and if there are any differences.

CHAPTER SIX

Finding the Healer Within

There is only one temple in the world and that is the human body. Nothing is more sacred than that noble form.

—Novalis

The brain minds the body. This idea seems so simple and central to the understanding of human health, and yet it has escaped the attention of the mainstream of medical practice and psychological thought. Medicine has largely regarded the body as a mindless machine.

—Ornstein and Sobel
The Healing Brain

What a man thinks, that he becomes; that is the eternal mystery.

—The Upanishads

People heal with their own minds . . . that's where the power is. Once you tap into it, you have joined up with a universal energy force. And with that power, nothing is impossible.

—Gerald Jampolsky, M.D.
The Complete Guide to Your Emotions & Your Health: New Dimensions in Mind/Body Healing

This chapter will offer tools for tapping into your own healing powers. Before you read on, however, I'd like to emphasize again that *I do not advise abandoning professional medical care. The techniques described in this book are simply suggestions.* Although they have been used successfully by my students and clients for stress reduction and health maintenance, *do not expect these exercises to be a panacea or instant cure.*

We usually associate physical illness with disease or injury to a specific body part or system. Disease is seen as an attack from an outsider with little concern for the mind's influence on the body's condition. In his groundbreaking book, *Mind as Healer, Mind as Slayer,* Kenneth Pelletier describes the current predicament of western medicine:

> Traditional medical practitioners have tended to limit their attention to the purely physical manifestations of disease and to avoid or discount the role of stress and emotions in physical pathology.

Our myopic view has prevented us from seeing that this split of body from mind is relatively recent in human history. Dr. Bernie Siegel, a well-known physician and surgeon, gives a larger perspective in his book, *Love, Medicine & Miracles*:

> Neglect of the mind-body link by technological medicine is actually a brief aberration when viewed against the whole history of the healing art. In traditional tribal medicine and in Western practice from its beginning in the work of Hippocrates, the need to operate through the patient's mind has always been recognized. Until the nineteenth century, medical writers rarely failed to note the influence of grief, despair, or discouragement on the onset and outcome of illness, nor did they ignore the healing effects of faith, confidence, and peace of mind.

A similar situation has occurred in the Eastern world where, for a relatively brief time, Western medical technology supplanted ancient systems of health and healing based on body/mind unity. These older traditions are being revived in both the East and the West. Examples of this resurgence can be seen in the spread of Chinese acupuncture and acupressure, herbal medicine, and Tai Chi Chuan, as well as Indian Ayurvedic medicine, Hatha Yoga, and meditation. The principles of body/mind unity stated in the previous quotes are echoed in this poetic passage from an ancient Indian text, the *Yoga-Vasistha*:

> The pains that afflict the body are called the *secondary diseases,* whilst the Vasanas (feelings and desires) that affect the mind are termed *primary or mental diseases. . . .*
>
> When the mind is agitated, then the body also follows in its wake. And when the body is agitated, then there is no proper perception of the things that are in one's way and prana (vital force) flies from its even path onto the bad road, staggering like an animal wounded by an arrow. Through such agitations, prana, instead of pervading the whole body steadily and equally, vibrates everywhere at an unequal rate. Therefore the nadis (subtle channels for prana) do not maintain a steady position, but quiver. Then to the body, which is the receptacle of food digested partially or completely, the nadis are simply death, because of the fluctuation of the pranas. The food which settles down in this body amidst such commotion is transformed into incurable diseases. Thus through the primary cause (of the mind) the disease of the body is generated. If this primary cause be annihilated at its root then all diseases will be destroyed.

If the agitated mind is the primary cause of disease in the body, what is it that causes the agitated mind? A Western physician, Dr. Brugh Joy, addresses this question in his book on transformational healing entitled *Joy's Way.* In speaking of most Western therapeutic approaches to the mind-body relationship, he writes:

> . . . hardly any of them accept experientially the body-mind-soul integrity. A mind cut off from the very source of its essence, the soul, is like a body cut off from its brain. In coma, or when portions of the brain are destroyed through anoxia, trauma, or destructive disease processes, the body still functions to a very limited degree and can be viable for long periods of time; but it is never anywhere near to complete functioning. In a similar way, the mind cut off from the soul is viable and can function in very limited degrees. Clearly,

> the soul that animates the mind is analogous to the mind that animates the body. When all three are in conjunction, the Transformational Process of the human being is greatly accelerated.

This body-mind-soul unity is the basis of what is now called holistic medicine. Pelletier has offered a detailed definition and framework for holistic medicine, as follows:

> Drawing upon numerous sources, it is possible to formulate several criteria for a fundamental working definition for holistic medicine. *First, all states of health and all disorders are considered to be psychosomatic. . . .*
>
> *Second, and related to this, is that each individual is unique and represents a complex interaction of body, mind, spirit. . . .*
>
> *Third is the fact that the patient and the health practitioners share the responsibility for the healing process.*
>
> Growing out of this third point is a *fourth aspect of holistic medicine: Health care is not exclusively the province or responsibility of orthodox medicine.* Diagnosis and treatment of pathology is obviously a medical concern, but the creation of a lifestyle conducive to health maintenance and personal fulfillment is beyond the limited scope of pathology correction.
>
> A fifth characteristic of holistic medicine is seeing illness as a creative opportunity for the patient to learn more about himself and his fundamental values. Illness needs to be viewed within the context of the entire life span of the patient.
>
> A sixth and final consideration of holistic medicine is that the practitioner must come to know himself as a human being. Anyone in a healing profession must become acquainted with his own emotional nature, his personality conflicts, his strengths and weaknesses, and generally to engage in a process of self-exploration. . . .

If a man becomes what he thinks, if the primary cause of disease is the agitated mind, and the "attackers" from without are the secondary cause, then the individual's mind holds great power over sickness as well as healing and health. According to Siegel:

> The modern medicine man has gained so much power over certain diseases through drugs that he has forgotten about the potential strength within the patient.

Dr. Joan Borysenko agrees. She is co-founder and director of the Body/Mind Clinic at New England Deaconess Hospital and Instructor in Medicine at Harvard Medical School. In her book, *Minding the Body, Mending the Mind,* she writes:

> Recent major studies indicate that approximately seventy-five percent of visits to the doctor are either for illnesses that will ultimately get better by themselves or for disorders related to anxiety and stress. For these conditions, symptoms can be reduced or cured as the body's own natural healing balance is reinstated.

Holistic medicine and Transformational Healing place the patient squarely at the center of the healing process. Yet how does this translate into practical measures when faced with such situations as the growing spread of AIDS (Acquired Immune Deficiency Syndrome) and AIDS-related diseases? Borysenko, who is married to an immunologist, writes about the "rich and intricate two-way communication system linking the mind, the immune system, and potentially all other systems, a pathway through which our emotions—our hopes and fears—can affect the body's ability to defend itself."

The next question that comes to mind is: How do we strengthen the immune system? How do we become strong from within? Dr. James Pennebaker, Professor of Psychology at Southern Methodist University, has done some research that points in a fascinating direction. He and his associates have discovered that the verbal (spoken and written) expression of feelings about an illness or trauma actually strengthens the immune system.

In a five-day study of fifty adults, Pennebaker found that those who wrote both facts and feelings about a critical health problem strengthened their immune systems and made fewer doctor visits. In this study, Pennebaker and Psychologist Janice Krecolt-Glaser told half the group to write out their feelings about their physical discomforts or illness, and the other half to write on superficial topics. Afterward, blood tests revealed that those who wrote about their illness showed greater improvement in their immune function than those who wrote on trivial subjects. Pennebaker reported to an annual American Psychological Association meeting that those who recorded their traumatic experience in diaries, journals, or letters made fewer doctor visits and enjoyed better overall health.

These findings certainly validate my own personal experiences, as described in the Introduction and Chapter One. Furthermore, in my work with art therapy clients and journal students, I have observed that both writing and *drawing* about an illness have a healing effect. In conversation, Dr. Pennebaker and I discovered a common interest in "therapeutic" drawing and its healing effects. Naturally, I am anxious to know of any research into the healing power of "right-brain" non-verbal forms of expression (drawing, painting, and sculpting) in which the emphasis is on the art *process* rather than performance or product.

For the purposes of this book, however, I will focus primarily on writing as a tool for self-healing. In working with several thousand individuals over a period of fourteen years, I discovered that parts of the body and diseases were actually trying to "speak" through physical symptoms. In their own mute but powerful language, the body parts and systems were trying to tell us something. The symptoms—irritations, soreness, inflammation, stiffness, congestion, aches, and pains—were all forms of thwarted expression.

First, I discovered how to listen to my own body by letting it write with my non-dominant hand. Whenever I did this a deep source of wisdom came through, decoding the messages, explaining the causes of the pain or disease, and telling me in no uncertain terms what to do about it. Then I shared this technique with others, and it worked for many of them, too. I was staggered by the simplicity of it. In essence, *the body part or symptom became both patient and healer, diagnosing the condition and prescribing its own cure!*

In the first *Well-Being Journal* class which I taught at a local YWCA, I saw immediate results. By this time I had received a Master's Degree in psychology and gone into private practice as an art therapist. In the class I guided students through techniques for keeping a journal or diary for personal growth. After doing right/left hand dialogues, some reported improvements and others experienced complete relief from chronic symptoms. Perhaps the most graphic and dramatic example is Pamela. In her case, one dialogue had a healing effect on a lifelong physical condition.

Pamela, an attractive young woman in her early thirties, joined my *Well-Being Journal* class because she wanted to write. She would have preferred the Creative Journal course, she said, but it wasn't being offered that semester. As it turned out, the *Well-Being* work was *exactly* what she needed. Here is Pamela's account of what happened:

> About twenty-five women of all ages sat in a circle as Lucia began the class by sharing her discovery of the therapeutic value of journal-keeping. I was surprised to find that she was absolutely open and honest, sharing her own personal experience of healing through writing and drawing. Her attitude established a completely safe and free atmosphere for us to simply be ourselves.
>
> The first question Lucia asked us to answer in our journals was, "How do you feel right now?" She explained that most people take that to mean emotions. She went on to say that she was talking not only about a state of mind, but physical sensations as well. How did we feel in every part of our bodies? She then guided us to listen to our bodies. My body was not feeling well at all. I was suffering from a chronic sinus

allergy I'd had since childhood which prevented normal breathing and was causing sore throats and headaches. Lucia encouraged us to respond to the questions by using our tools, a blank book and colored felt pens. We were to draw and write our answers to the "How do you feel?" question right there and then. She also urged us to do assigned exercises at home.

Although I felt quite resistant to the idea, I finally took her advice one day and went into a secluded room in my home. Pen in hand, I asked the question, "How are you?" of my poor aching sinuses. Then I put the felt pen in my "other hand," which for me was my left hand. In bold, scrawling red, I received an answer from my sinuses: "I really want my mommy!" A torrent of tears followed this revelation and I experienced an intense emotional release. I felt four years old again. In a few short minutes I relieved and released the sadness I had felt at age four when my mother left me to live with my grandmother.

Here is Pamela's complete dialogue, with left-hand writing in italics:

Pamela, how do you feel?

Fine except my head (sinases), my eyes itch & hurt so much. I really want my mommy. My chest hurts & feels dusty inside. It used to feel tight like I couldn't breathe but now it just feels dusty.

You're really a big baby, you know.

No I'm not. I want to be well.

What can I do for you?

Let me talk to you. I miss you and I need you so much. You've been very mean to me for so long. I'm so sad. I just feel so dirty like in my lungs. Not lungs—those long things. They hurt so much. My eyes feel weak & lonely, itch & my holes in my head are plugged with milk. I don't like milk.

Pamela how do you feel?

Fine except my head (sinases), mey eyes itcht hurt so much. I really want my mommy.

Do you feel better now? I'm so sorry, my baby, for all of this. I didn't know. I didn't have any idea how you felt.

I still want my mommy. Give her back.

This dialogue helped Pamela see that, as an adult, she now had the power and responsibility to re-parent her own abandoned and hurt Inner Child. As she activated a nurturing, compassionate part of herself, she began the process of healing. After her discovery in this dialogue, Pamela's allergies gradually vanished and have not returned.

If you have a chronic physical problem or symptom whose nature and cause you want to explore, then do the following exercise. It is designed to help you listen more carefully to physical sensations and also to hear the wisdom in your body.

BODY TALKS

Materials: paper, set of felt tip pens in assorted colors.

1. Sit quietly, focus inward. Get in touch with a body part that is painful or dis-eased.
2. Draw an outline of your entire body. Then, in color, draw in that body part. (If you're not sure what it looks like or think you can't render it correctly, just use your imagination.) In your picture, color the painful or diseased part. Use colors that express how the body part feels. For instance, if the pain is a burning sensation, use a "hot" color like red or orange. If there's a lump or other distortion to the body part, include it in your drawing.
3. Interview the body part by writing questions with your dominant hand. Let the body part or disease write the answers with the non-dominant hand. Use two different colors, one for each hand.

Ask the following questions:

A. Who are you? or What are you?

B. How do you feel?

C. What caused you to feel this way?

D. How can I help you? What do you want me to do for you?

Observe any new understandings of what may be causing your discomfort or illness. Have you gained any insights into what part you can play in the healing process?

The following story is a classic case of successful healing through medical treatment combined with right/left hand dialogues. When I met Erin, she was in her mid-twenties, a bright, outgoing young woman shopping for a career. She had a degree in art and was interested in becoming an art therapist. Like Pamela, she came in for career advancement but went out with tools for healing herself.

Over many months of journal-writing and drawing in my classes, Erin experienced a recurring theme: a chronic bladder infection (for which she was receiving medical treatment). In retrospect she described her healing experience as follows:

> Somehow, I always knew that if I had a physical problem and could decode what it was trying to tell me, I could clear the problem up. Everytime I drew a picture of how my bladder felt and then conversed with it, issues would come up. I started the process of looking at things about myself and my life that I hadn't wanted to look at.
>
> The biggest problem was a friend with whom I was having great difficulty. In my dialogues, it became very clear that this person was not healthy for me. But I still had to struggle with what to do about it.

> My doctor at that time was a well-known physician who practices holistic medicine. That is, he takes life situations into account when diagnosing and prescribing a "cure." Since I had gotten in touch with the problem friendship in my journal writing, I was able to talk more freely about it. After hearing what I said, the doctor finally said to me: "This person is causing your bladder problem. If you want to heal it, drop this so-called friendship." I knew he was right. He confirmed what my dialogue had said. His words really got through to me. I finally dropped that person from my life and when I did my bladder problem disappeared.
>
> What I've learned from all this is that my body goes out of whack when I'm doing something I shouldn't be doing. It tells me I'm on the wrong track. For me, this usually involves a friendship that doesn't nurture me, a relationship that is not healthy. If I stay in those non-nurturing relationships, I break out in rashes or develop infections.

Another student who started a deep inner healing process through dialogues with a physical discomfort is Jill. As a child, Jill wanted to become an actress when she grew up. But emotionally she wasn't able to follow through with her childhood dream and take it into adulthood. Instead she did what was expected of her, got married and had children. As she puts it, she became "Mrs. Somebody" and "Somebody's Mother."

After years of taking care of everyone else while ignoring her dream, Jill took a stand. She started seeing a therapist and also took one of my weekend journal workshops, where she discovered the healing power of her Inner Child through a right/left-hand dialogue. "It was a major breakthrough in my life," she recounts. Her first dialogue was a conversation with her headache. As she wrote, she soon contacted the Little Girl within who had been silenced for so many years.

Who are you?

YOUR HEAD

How do you feel?

I FEEL PESSURE

Why do you feel this - Are you saying pressure or pleasure?

PLEASURE CREATES PRESSURE

Do you feel guilty when you are too happy?

I FEEL SCARED THAT SOMETHING WILL HAPPEN SO IF I HURT IT CAN'T HAPPEN.

You hurt a little now. Would you like to tell me why?

BRAIN FEELS NICE FEELING NICE IS BAD

HEADACHE DIALOGUE

(italics: non-dominant hand)

Who are you?

Your head.

How do you feel?

I feel pessure.

Why do you feel this—are you saying pressure or pleasure?

Pleasure creates pressure.

Do you feel guilty when you are too happy?

I feel scared that something will happen so if I hurt it can't happen.

You hurt a little now. Would you like to tell me why?

Brain feels nice feeling nice is bad.

No, it is not nice to feel bad. It is not bad to feel nice. Who told you that?

Mommy said don't like your body it is naughty to love yourself.

Mommy was wrong about that. Anyhow she is not around any more.

Yes she is in me I am her in your head.

Can I do something to help you so you won't hurt?

Yes you can tell me not to be afraid.

There is nothing to be afraid of. I will help you. I will take care of you. But I get angry sometimes.

If you are angry Mommy won't like you.

If Mommy doesn't like me because I get angry, then she doesn't understand. We can't control someone who doesn't understand.

It is OK to be angry but we need to find a way to express it that doesn't hurt you.

I am afraid.

What are you afraid of? Can I help you?

I want to be free.

What would you do if you were free?

I would hit and bite and scream.

Maybe we can go into a room by ourselves and do this. Would you like that?

Yes.

Are there other ways you can express yourself without really hurting anyone else?

I want to dance.

Years ago we used to play music and dance when we were alone —would you like that?

Yes I don't care how I look. You care how I look. You make trouble for me. You tell me I am clumsy. I want to be graceful but I am scared and scarred.

You have scars from the freeway accident. Is that why? Does all this go that far back?

Everybody always said use your head. I scarred myself to get attention because I am special and I wanted you to know me.

Were the migraine headaches a way of getting attention, then, too?

You wouldn't use me so I had to remind you. I want to think and feel together. You are Libra the balance. I am unbalanced you have to balance me.

How can I do that?

You must love me and respect me. I feel and think too, not just thinking.

Are you saying that I didn't consider your feelings enough?

You want to be a thinking head only feel somewhere else. Not right. Head does think and feel both. You say feel is bad so I feel bad.

If you believe feeling is good, would you feel good?

That is not exactly right.

What would make you feel good? I notice you hurt now.

That's right I hurt. Let me cry. Daddy never let me cry. I know Daddy isn't here any more but you sometimes carry him around. I want to cry when I'm sad.

I will let you cry when you're sad. I will try not to worry what people think or say. I will love you even if you hurt.

That's right. I only hurt to get your attention. I love you and want to work for you but you need to listen to what I'm feeling. I will give you warning signs. Tune in. Listen.

I feel more relaxed now. I will try to work with you.

Don't try. We already have too much trying. Just be you and I'll be me and not what someone else wants. Just let me flow in to the stream that is the bloodstream and I will be in natural rhythm if you don't disturb it. You pick on me too much. Leave me be and let me flow the way I am supposed to. Goodbye.

Jill's dialogue ended with this drawing.

Colors on drawing:
outline—golden tan
lines inside and writing—red

Right hand wrote in black ink throughout.

Left hand wrote in brown ink. Starting with "That is not exactly right," it switched to blue-green ink.

In this dialogue, Jill (the adult) became a Wise Counselor and Nurturing Parent to her own Inner Child, who was "trapped" in her headache. She discovered that she had played victim all her life. Actually her Inner Child was the victim and by repressing its existence she had unwittingly perpetuated her own limitations. She decided to stop being a victim, started paying attention to her own goals and following through with them. Jill studied acting, became a professional, and has appeared on television. It all started with a headache, but it led to making her dreams come true.

There is another kind of healing that has to do with self/body image: healing attitudes about parts of our bodies that we don't like. As we grow up, we are criticized for certain physical traits or we compare ourselves to current models or ideals of attractiveness and conclude that we don't measure up. Many people direct self-condemnation and low self-esteem to specific body parts. How many times have you heard, "I hate my nose," or "My hair is horrible," or "It's hopeless, I'll never lose all this fat." Self-put-downs show up in poor posture, extra weight, wrinkles, chronic physical problems or symptoms. We believe that one part of our body is weak, ugly, awkward. We identify with that part and judge it (and ourselves). Weak, ugly, awkward? Familiar words? Yes, all the words used to describe the left hand, as documented in Chapter Two.

Here is a chance to get to the root of low self-esteem as it lives in your body and heal it. The next exercise will let you see and "hear" any negative attitudes you are embodying, so that you can let go of them. You will visualize your body by drawing a picture of it. This will enable you to identify the specific "problem" area and dialogue with it. In this way you can begin healing the attitude that has caused your poor self-image.

BODY TALKS BACK

Materials: Paper, felt pens in assorted colors

1. With your dominant hand make a list of the parts of your body that you dislike.
2. Choose one part from your list. Draw a picture of it in color.
3. Using your non-dominant hand, let the body part speak and tell how it feels and what it wants.
4. With your dominant hand, respond to what the body part needs and wants. Tell it what you will do to take care of it and love it.

Elizabeth attended one of my journal seminars in which I assigned the *Body Talks Back* exercise. She focused on the latest scourge of modern women, cellulite (those little globules of fatty substance that form on the stomach, hips, thighs and buttocks). She drew a picture and let the cellulite talk (in a monologue) with her non-dominant hand.

Hi! It's me, your happy friendly, soft cellulite. You don't like me very much . . . but you've never asked me to go away. You've been hanging onto me here for three or four years now. Why?

No answer, huh?

A little self-destruction, maybe? A little self-pity?

You know what? I don't think the answer is important enough now—I really don't think the answer has a name!

Isn't that wonderful? For both of us!

Now I can finally transform to strong, useable skin tissue—and you can let me go. Come on! You can't even remember why I'm here! Sometimes you're so silly.

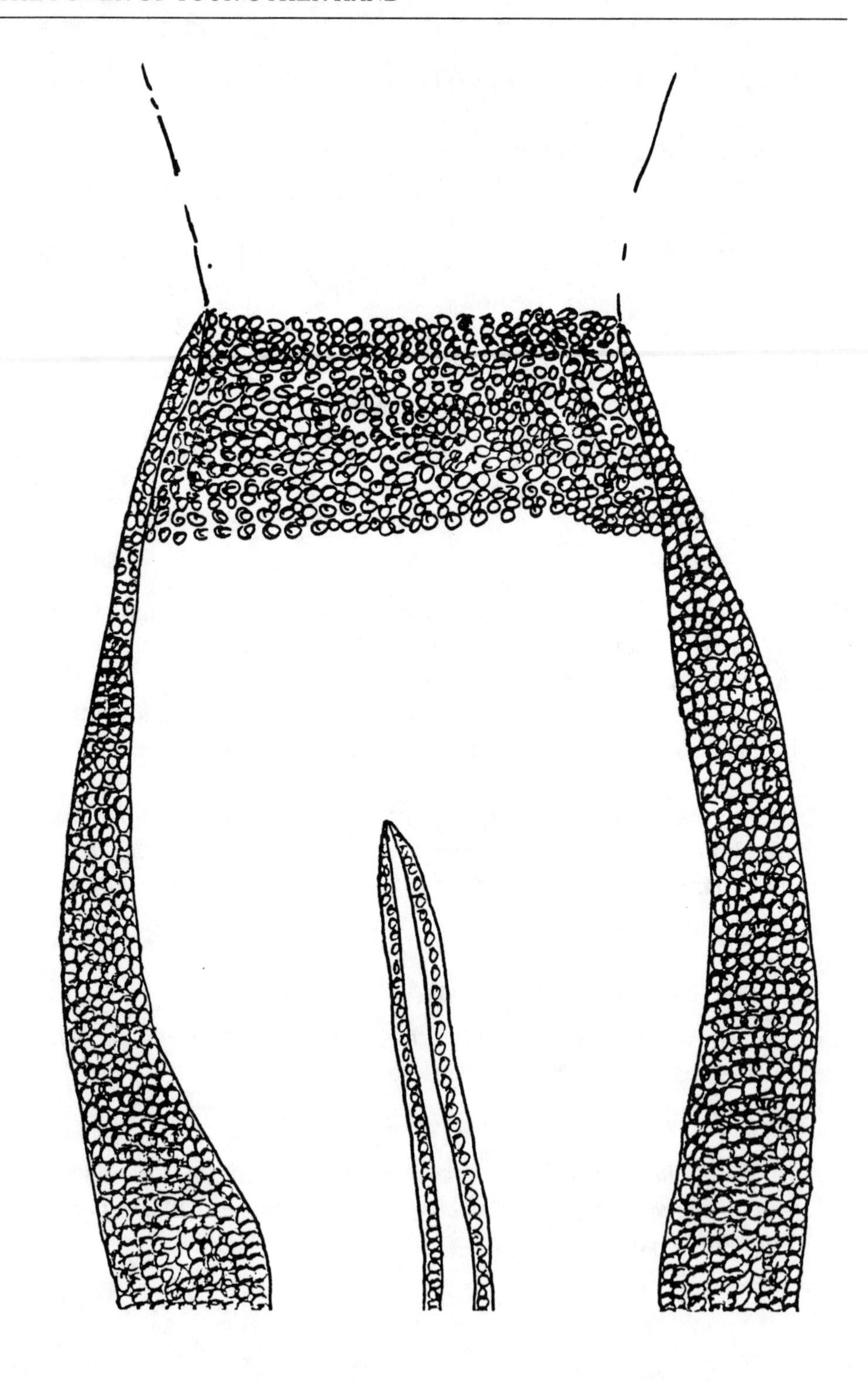

Her drawing and dialogue with cellulite launched Elizabeth into a series of life changes which included a permanent weight loss of thirty-five pounds, and a career change in which she became a journal teacher and writer of "how-to" books. She has recently co-authored with me, *Lighten Up Journal: Making Friends With Your Body.*

The following is another headache dialogue. This one was written by Dorothy, a school teacher. It shows clearly how attitudes and feelings hide out in body parts and symptoms. The headache is speaking with the *non-dominant* hand and is shown here in italics.

> (Dominant) Well, headache, there you are again. Why are you here?
>
> *(Non-dominant) I'm doing my job protecting you, keeping the ugliness out.*
>
> What ugliness?
>
> *The ugliness that you don't want to face, the reality that you're not perfect. You have weaknesses; you're vulnerable; you need other people. You can't exist alone, a self-entity not needing anyone.*
>
> But I've reached out and been hurt.
>
> *The only hurt you've received is of your own making. You've criticized yourself, abused yourself. You've hurt yourself* more than all *the other people combined. Isn't it about time you stopped doing that to yourself?*
>
> I guess so, but it just seems easier to not think about it, be mad, and create a headache.
>
> *You know what? You're being perfect, all right. You're being a perfect headache to yourself. You're like a big, fat, solid roadblock in your own road. You're so angry at yourself for not being perfect you set up roadblocks for yourself so you'll get confused and stuck and maybe fail. That way you can prove you're not perfect. Is that a very smart, loving thing to do?*

No, maybe I'd better stop it. It isn't serving me well. It's keeping me little. I want to grow up.

Then deal *with things instead of hiding behind physical symptoms!*

By now it should be clear that healing comes from within, from a core of wisdom, understanding and compassion that resides deep inside the Self. And perhaps there is no healing so profound nor so basic as the healing of the Inner Child, as demonstrated in Pamela's dialogue with her head and Jill's conversation with her headache.

It is my experience that physical pain and many illnesses are the hidden Inner Child crying out for love and attention. This Inner Child is our child-like feeling state—fear, shyness, sadness, excitement, joy, playfulness. We all carry such feelings around inside, but learn to shut them off as we grow up. We have adopted the ways of adulthood: work, practicality, and reason. Our child-selves—feelings, intuitions, creativity—have been denied. But the child in us is so much a part of our life force that it *must* find a way out. If it can't come out naturally, it will force its way out in distorted forms called illness, disease, fatigue, depression, or even violence. The next chapter has tools for this deepest, yet most rewarding task: healing your Inner Child.

CHAPTER SEVEN

Recovery of the Inner Child

Ah, but I was so much older then,
I'm younger than that now.

—Bob Dylan
"My Back Pages"

It takes a long time to become young.

—Pablo Picasso

I'm your very own child and I live inside you. And I'll never grow up and go away. I'll always be here.

—Lucia's Inner Child
printed with her left hand

Child abuse is a downward spiral, a tragic affliction handed down from one generation to the next. It has always existed, but we've heard more about it in recent years through media coverage. It may have gotten worse or it may simply be that we are willing to bring it out in the open now. And we are shocked at what we find: psychological torment, physical and sexual abuse in families and in schools, child pornography, and kidnapping. More and more children are escaping into gangs, drugs, and sometimes even suicide.

Since the beginning of modern psychotherapy, the issue of childhood trauma has been a central factor in many methods of treatment. More recently, in the writings of psychoanalyst Alice Miller, we learn how society breeds psychopathology and violence in the home, school, and other institutions. In childhood, most of us were abused to one degree or another. Those of us who have worked as therapists with adults, adolescents, or children will attest to the grim fact that many people prefer to deny the deplorable treatment they received in their early years—the neglect, cooercion, or outright violation—in favor of a fantasy memory of "happy childhood." As long as the denial continues, there is no way to "work through" the abuse, so it is passed down to the next generation.

Denial has been a key issue in the families of alcoholics/addicts/obsessive-compulsives. The denial of family problems was so great that, in the case of adult children of alcoholics, it isn't until many years after leaving home that the truth is allowed to surface, sometimes overwhelming the individual with pain, grief, and rage. The problem in the U.S. has reached staggering proportions. In his excellent book, *Healing the Child Within: Discovery and Recovery for Adult Children of Dysfunctional Families*, Charles Whitfield, M.D. writes that new self-help groups for adult children of alcoholics were forming (in the late '80s) at a rate of one per day. These are non-professional, no-fee organizations patterned after the highly successful twelve-step program of Alcoholics Anonymous and Alanon. As a participant in these programs, I can personally attest to their effectiveness. They have given hope to the hopeless and strength to the helpless.

In the fields of psychotherapy, social work, and education, more and more professionals are addressing the problem of child abuse. And in counseling work with adults, the theme of healing the Inner Child is being presented in books, workshops, seminars, and professional training programs. If Whitfield is correct in his estimation that 80 to 95% of the population did not receive adequate parenting, then healing the Inner Child becomes a task for most of us.

Starting in the '60s and '70s, Hugh Missildine (*Your Child of the Past*) and Eric Berne (*Transactional Analysis*) introduced the concept of the Inner Child. In the '80s, Miller, Whitfield, and Stone and Winkelman have continued with books and therapeutic techniques for finding and healing the Child Within. These experts are all in agreement that there is a Child still living in all of us, a Child who continues to need parenting. But we must become our own parents. We must provide the understanding, compassion and guidance of a parent for our own Inner Child.

This Inner Child consists of all our child-like feelings, instincts, intuitions, spontaneity, and vitality. It is naturally open and trusting unless it learns to shut down for self-protection. It is emotional and expressive until condemned for being what it is—a child. It is playful until it is crushed for being childish. This Inner Child is creative until ridiculed for its expression. It is magical until it is punished for using its imagination. We can bury it, distort it, handicap it, make it sick, but we can't get rid of it.

By the time most of us reach adulthood, our natural, healthy child-like traits are so wounded they are nearly dead. Or they are distorted beyond recognition. Alcoholism, drug addiction, sexual obsession, eating disorders, compulsive spending, and gambling are some of the misguided attempts to return to childhood. The behavior that results is inappropriate childishness rather than true child-likeness.

Hal Stone and Sidra Winkelman write poignantly about

> the loss of the Inner Child. . . one of the most profound tragedies of the "growing-up" process. We lose so much of the magic and mystery of living. We lose so much of the delight and intimacy of relationship. So much of the destructiveness that we bring to each other as human beings is a function of our lack of connection to our sensitivities, our fears, our own magic. . . . perhaps the most universally disowned self in our civilized world is the Vulnerable Child. Yet this Vulnerable Child may be our most precious sub-personality—the closest to our essence—the one that enables us to become truly intimate, to fully experience others, and to love.

But there is hope. The Child doesn't die. It's still in there and it can be contacted and revived. As Charles Whitfield puts it:

> Our Child Within flows naturally from the time we are born to the time that we die and during all of our times and transitions in between. We don't have to do anything . . . It just is. If we simply let it be, it will express itself with no particular effort on our part. Indeed, any effort is usually in denying our awareness and expression of it.

And where does this Child live? In our feelings, hunches, likes and dislikes, our wishes and dreams, our fantasies and wildest imaginings. The exercises in this chapter (and throughout this book) are designed to help you find, understand, and love that Child Within: the Vulnerable Child, the Playful Child, the Magical Child, and all the other subtle nuances of feeling which this part of you contains. You will learn techniques for recovery from the abuses of childhood.

First, you'll have an opportunity to spend some time getting acquainted with your Inner Child. You will discover who that aspect of your personality really is, what it likes and doesn't like, how it feels, and what it needs. You will also have a chance to accept and nurture your Inner Child in a mutually beneficial way. You may even come home to the joy of the Inner Child.

GETTING TO KNOW YOUR INNER CHILD

1. Picture a place you feel would be comfortable for your Inner Child, such as:
   near a lake, river or ocean
   in a meadow
   in a garden
   in a beautiful room.

2. Now invite your Inner Child to come into the picture. See this child in your mind's eye and ask yourself, Is it a boy or girl? How old? What does the child look like?

3. Now start writing out a dialogue. Writing with your dominant hand, greet the child, introduce yourself and ask his or her name. Let your Inner Child respond by writing with the *other hand.*

4. Tell the child you want to get to know his or her feelings, needs, likes, and dislikes. Then continue the conversation. The Nurturing Parent writes with the dominant hand, the Inner Child with the non-dominant hand.

5. Complete your conversation by asking the Inner Child for one special thing it wants from you. Work out something that is mutually agreeable, that satisfies the Child's needs as well as those of the Nurturing Parent, who is responsible for following through. Make sure you are willing to keep the agreement made to the Child. If not, don't make any promises, otherwise you will disappoint the Child and cause further hurt.

6. Thank the Child for coming out. If you are willing to meet again, agree on a place and time.

In your everyday life notice the times when you feel child-like. What do you do about it? Do you observe the feelings and let them be? Are you uncomfortable with the feelings? Do you push them away?

In 1986 I came across Hal Stone and Sidra Winkelman's book entitled, *Embracing Our Selves.* It describes their method of therapy known as Voice Dialogue. Rooted in Jungian work, Gestalt Therapy, Transactional Analysis, and Psychodrama, Voice Dialogue enables the individual to converse out loud with a broad range of sub-personalities. It also opens up the "awareness level," or the Inner Witness, who observes without judgment.

Within two days of reading *Embracing Our Selves,* I found myself in a private therapy session with Hal Stone. Hal "directed" my inner drama by having me move around the room and act out several different sub-personalities. Their names describe them accurately: the Controller/Protector, my Vulnerable Child, the Nurturing Mother (whose name is "Mama Lucia"), and my Play Girl. Each character in my inner drama had its own place in the room, its own body language, and its own distinct voice. Like the handwriting of sub-personalities in my journals, the physical expression of each part of myself was unique.

When I spoke from my Vulnerable Child in my first Voice Dialogue session, I was reminded of my very first therapy session thirteen years before. At that time I sat on the floor and regressed to early childhood as I printed awkwardly with my left hand. It seemed that no matter what I did, how much I learned, I always came back to the same place: the Child Within. She never grew up, she never went away, she was still there, waiting to be healed.

Later I entered weekly therapy with Hal's wife, Sidra, and the drama unfolded. I confronted parts of myself (feeling states and personality traits) which I feared or hated or overvalued. Some of these parts had seemed foreign to me before I "owned" them in these dialogues. One of these "shadows" called himself a "shady character"and spoke like a Mafia type. There were other parts of myself with which I overidentified at that time, like the Mama Lucia character who took care of everyone else except my Vulnerable Child. In doing these enactments, I was given tools for removing my projections onto others and acknowledging those very qualities in myself. Voice Dialogue also helped me to hold the opposites within myself: the soft, sensitive side along with the assertive, "in-charge" side, the creative aspects as well as the self-destructive ones. And it helped me, once again, to get back in touch with the *other hand.*

A week after my first Voice Dialogue session, I sat down and wrote a conversation. I started to cry as I wrote the last words, "I'll never grow up and go away." One of the issues I'd been dealing with in my personal life was the fact that my younger daughter, Aleta, was planning to move away from home. It was not a decision born from conflict. In

Dear Vulnerable Child, I'm so glad I found you again. Is there anything you'd like to say to me today?

YES. I WANT YOU TO STAY WITH ME. AND TAKE ME WITH YOU WHEREVER YOU GO. PLEASE LISTEN TO MY FEELINGS AND TAKE CARE OF ME. DON'T LET THOSE OTHER ONES DROWN ME OUT OR BE MEAN TO ME. DON'T LET THEM TALK YOU INTO TRYING TO LEAVE ME OUT 'CAUSE YOU CAN'T LEAVE ME OUT. I'M YOUR VERY OWN CHILD AND I LIVE INSIDE YOU. AND I'LL NEVER GROW UP AND GO AWAY. I'LL ALWAYS BE HERE.

fact, we had arrived at a very nourishing and mutually supportive relationship that is rare between parent and child. But she was twenty-three and it was time for her to have her own place. We had both accepted that. We were taking the next step in her growth and mine. And yet, I was feeling sadness at the ending of an era in my life. I feared the unknown and loneliness.

The dialogue with my Vulnerable Child helped me see that I would not be alone. I would not be a childless mother. My Inner Child was being born (again) and she needed my attention. She wanted a new, transformed relationship with me.

The next exercise will enable you to meet your Vulnerable Child. Since the Vulnerable Child does not fit with the "adult" image, this might be the disowned part of you. It is probably buried pretty deep. But as we have seen, letting it write with your non-dominant hand will give it a chance to come out more easily. It may take a little more time, but it will be well worth it, as you will discover for yourself. The energy and vitality that results from these dialogues is quite remarkable.

HEALING YOUR VULNERABLE CHILD

1. Visualize a very safe place, an environment that is sheltered and soothing, such as a cozy little room with soft furniture, or some other space that feels warm and inviting.
2. Picture your Vulnerable Child in detail: age, gender, appearance, place in the room or environment you've created.
3. Greet and invite the Child to be with you. Write out your conversation, using both hands. The Nurturing Self writes with your dominant hand, the Vulnerable Child with the non-dominant.
4. Ask your Vulnerable Child the following questions:
   Who are you?
   How do you feel?

Why do you feel that way?
What can I do to help you?

5. Tell your Vulnerable Child exactly what you will do to follow through, and meet its needs. If you can't, don't make any promises. This will betray your Child's trust and only make matters worse.

6. If you want to visit with your Vulnerable Child again, agree on a place and time. Then thank your Child for coming out and say good-bye for now.

Notice in your everyday life when your Vulnerable Child is present. This usually happens when you experience fatigue, sickness, fear, sadness, shyness, disappointment. Observe what you do with these feelings. Do you allow yourself to truly feel them? Do you block them out with food, drugs, alcohol, extra work, oversocializing, TV?

Just as it is possible to establish a rapport with the Vulnerable Child who lives in us today, it is also possible to heal the Child of the Past. One of my students who healed his Vulnerable Child of the Past is Tom, a distinguished-looking middle-aged medical doctor and counseler. He attended my weekly journal-keeping class for himself, but also to learn methods to use with his patients, especially those who were hospitalized.

When Tom came to my class he thought he was right-handed. As it turned out, he was actually a switch-over (a natural lefty forced into right-handedness). There is no question in my mind that such coercion to conform to the "majority hand" does deep psychological damage to the individual's Vulnerable Child. But the wound can be healed in adulthood, as we will see in Tom's case.

When Tom was given permission to write with his left hand, he re-experienced a situation with his early teacher. While writing, he actually relived some painful events and later told the grim story. In his early childhood, a teacher had forced little Tom (through physical abuse and threats) into right-handedness. He had attempted to fight back, but the teacher won out. He saw the teacher as a witch and was able to feel the rage and frustration he had been forced to repress as a child in the adult's world. Later, he was able to forgive her by changing her from a witch into a woman (a human being who was doing the best she could). By doing this, Tom healed the childhood trauma of being forced to switch from his natural hand.

A few weeks after Tom started writing with his left hand, class members remarked that he smiled more and seemed far more relaxed. Several years later, this is how he described his left handwriting:

> My left handwriting is more graceful and is actually more legible than writing done with my right hand. I like it better. I write letters to others with my left hand. If I have time, I write any personal expression with my left hand. My right-hand writing is unpleasing to me now.

Tom's story had a happy ending: healing his Vulnerable Inner Child. Forced to renounce his left-handedness by a grown-up who was stronger and held authority, Little Tom was denied his natural style of expression. Big Tom finally rescued Little Tom by putting a pen in his natural hand and allowing him to speak.

The next exercise will enable you to revisit and heal a situation that may have overwhelmed you when you were a child. You will be collapsing time, so to speak, and bringing the past into the present moment. You will deal with a concrete situation, with specific feelings and reactions that were buried at the time. You will become your own counselor. This exercise can empower you to take responsibility for yourself instead of blaming your parents or others from your childhood. If there are still feelings alive in you from past situations, then the Inner Child is still alive. And *you*, the adult, are now its parent. It's up to you to give that Child the kindness and understanding it needs, instead of demanding that others do it for you.

HEALING YOUR CHILD OF THE PAST

1. Go back to a time in childhood when you were frightened, sad, lonely, or felt some very strong emotion that you couldn't express at the time.
2. Imagine that the adult of the present visits this Child of the Past and sits down to talk with it. Be the Child's counselor.
3. Have a conversation with the Inner Child of the Past. As a counselor, let the Child tell you about itself, what happened, and what it needs. Let the counselor write with your dominant hand; invite the Inner Child of the Past to write with your *other hand.* Ask the Inner Child the following questions:
   What's your name or nickname?
   How old are you?
   Tell me about yourself. What happened to you?
   How do you feel?
   Why do you feel that way?
   What do you need now? How can I help you?

Observe your feelings in everyday life. Watch to see if this Child of the Past comes out.

Over the years, many therapists, doctors, and teachers have applied these methods in their work. One of these is Molly. When she took my professional's training course, she was deeply moved by the right/left-hand dialogues. She seized upon this technique as a perfect vehicle for healing the Inner Child. Molly is now a counselor in private practice and also works in shelters for battered women and children. She specializes in healing the Inner Child.

Molly recommends that her clients keep a journal. In the safety and confidentiality of a personal journal or diary, her clients have been able to say things they couldn't say out loud. Molly helps her clients express their buried feelings and respond to their own path with compassion and nurturing. She reports great success with adults and children alike.

Here is the text of a deeply moving dialogue by an eleven-year-old sexually abused girl whom Molly counseled. The child wrote conversations with five different aspects of her personality, giving each one a descriptive name. She is right-handed, so her sub-personalities wrote through her left hand, indicated in italics.

1. *FROWNY*

Hello.

Hi.

What's your name?

Frowny.

How are you?

Sad, very sad and scared, I don't want to have to go to school. Scary.

Why are you scared?

Because I want a popie and all I had all my life was a mean cruel father. I want a home, a popie, a mommy, a doggie and a birdie. I want comfort and understanding and fun and love.

What can I do to help you?

Get me a house, a popie. I don't want my father, I want a popie and my dog and my mommy and my birdies. Please keep this. You know nobody understands. I want my mommy to understand what it's like not to ever have a popie and I don't like my father very much. I just want a popie.

What makes you happy?

A house, I want to go to the beach and movies I am so bored.

2. *MEENY*

Hello.

Hi.

What's your name?

Meeny.

How are you feeling?

Miserable!

Why?

Because.

What can I do for you?

Nothing, I just want to live in the house with Snookie [her dog].

What makes you happy?

Nothing. I just want to go to the beach, Disneyland, Marineland, live in the house with Mommy and Snookie.

What can I do for you?

Stop swats and get good grades and stop these problems. I want a house.

What makes you happy?

Disneyland and Magic Mountain, Sea World and Marineland. Then I can get away from problems, I can think then.

3. *BEAVER*

Hello.

Hi.

What's your name?

Beaver.

How are you feeling?

Fine. Well, I—I—so so.

Why?

Because I want to have fun!

What can I do for you?

Play, have fun, take me places, smile, laugh, get good grades, especially play. Please have fun stop letting Nerdy, Clowny, *and* Meeny *or* Frowny *out.*

What makes you happy?

Just plain fun and love.

4. *CLOWNY*

Hello.

Hi.

What's your name?

Clowny.

How are you feeling?

Better today. Most of the time I feel sad and scared.

Why?

Because I'm scared to get a swat and I want to get good grades.

What can I do for you?

Stop swats and get good grades and stop these problems. I want a house.

What makes you happy?

Disneyland and Magic Mountain, Sea World and Marineland. Then I can get away from problems. I can think then.

5. *NERDY*

Hello.

Hi.

What's your name?

Nerdy.

How are you feeling?

Afraid.

Why?

I don't know.

What can I do for you?

Don't be scared.

What makes you happy?

Amusement parks, my Gramma, Snookie, Mommy, and my house. Oh how I need my house, please my house.

As I described earlier, discovering my Inner Child was a turning point in my life. It was that Child Within that played a big part in my decision to become an art therapist. The Child in me made it possible to bring out the Child that lived in my clients and journal students. Through spontaneous drawing, modeling in clay, movement, and music, they contacted a source of healing, aliveness, and creativity that transformed their lives. On the one hand, I acted like a grown-up professional, but I always knew it was my Inner Child who "worked the magic."

An important aspect of the Inner Child that came out was the Playful Child. She loves to have fun, to be silly, to play "dress up," and also get messy. She helped me discover some long-buried childhood wishes, such as wanting to take dance lessons. After I began dancing, the Child wanted to roller skate (for the first time since I was a kid). The roller-skate craze had just begun, so I had lots of company. There were plenty of other adults with Inner Playful Children out skating, too. My Playful Child even got me into skateboarding at age thirty-nine! Another adult with an active Playful Child was the one who encouraged me to skateboard. This photo of me on my skateboard is a perfect example of what happens when your Playful Child is out. Boy, was that fun!

Giving your Playful Child a chance to come out will be especially valuable if you are one of the many adults who do not take the time to really play. Some adults don't even know *how* to play anymore. They mistake play for overeating or overdrinking, taking drugs, gambling, or shopping compulsively. Due to tremendous preoccupation with the adult "image" and responsibilities, many people have lost their ability to be *in the moment,* to enjoy simple pleasures, and to smell the roses.

The next exercise is intended to help you meet your Playful Child. This is the part of you that is genuinely fun-loving, spontaneous, and exuberant. It can be silly, have a sense of humor, and experience joy at being alive. The Playful Child is very present in the body and *in the moment.* It enjoys pleasurable sensations: beautiful colors, delicious tastes, the feel of an ocean breeze, moving the body in ways that are enjoyable, a hot bath on a cold day. The Playful Child doesn't do things because they're supposed to be "good for you." It does them because they feel good.

So send your "stuffy" grown-up on a brief vacation (the part of you that's all work and no play), and invite the Playful Child that lives inside you to come out.

PLAYFUL CHILD

1. Imagine an environment where your Playful Child would enjoy meeting with you, such as:
   a playroom
   a playground
   a zoo
   an amusement park or carnival

James Ruebsamen, *Evening Outlook*

the beach
recreation center.

2. Now invite the Child to come out and be with you. Let the Playful Child draw a picture of itself with your non-dominant hand. Ask the Child to tell you its name and print it on the picture.

3. Writing with your dominant hand (as your adult self), have a conversation with your Playful Child (who writes through your non-dominant hand). Ask the Child all about itself.
   What do you like? What don't you like?
   Where do you like to play?
   What kind of things do you like to do when you play?
   Who do you like to play with?
   What do you like to eat and drink?
   What are your favorite places to eat?
   Where do you like to go on vacation?
   What kind of clothes do you like to wear?
   What are your favorite colors?
   What is your favorite room? Favorite place?

4. Ask your Playful Child how it feels about its place in your life at this time. Does it feel wanted and included? Does it feel ignored and left out?

5. Ask your Playful Child for one thing it wants from you. If you are willing to do it, tell the Child exactly how you will meet its request. Be specific. If you are not going to follow through, don't make promises. This will only disappoint the Child and weaken the trust between you.

6. Thank your Playful Child for coming out to talk with you and agree to meet again if you are willing to do that.

Later on, be aware of the Playful Child when it wants to come out in your everyday life. It may want some time to take a hot bath or go to the park or pick a bunch of flowers or bike ride to the store instead of driving.

> The Magical Child is really a brother or sister to the Playful Child. It is the child of imagination and fantasy. It is the child of our right brain, or our intuition and creative imagination.
>
> —Hal Stone and Sidra Winkelman
> *Embracing Ourselves*

And who is this Magical Child? It is the creative part of us that enables us to be receptive to breakthroughs and new ways of seeing things. It is the part of us that "takes a break" from the adult, rational way of screening our experience through left-brain logic. The Magical Child dares to see and do things in unique and original ways. It has hunches, intuitions, and visions.

The Magical Child lives in our night dreams and day dreams and fantasies. It is the dreamer in us. It knows the world of imagination has as much "reality" as the physical world. It knows that the physical world started in imagination. The Magical Child believes in fairies and spirits because it *knows* there are other worlds, other realms than what our senses perceive. It talks to animals and flowers and it will "wish upon a star" because it knows it is one with all creation. It believes in the soul, in the unseen essence of things.

Now let's go on a journey to discover your Magical Child. This exercise is designed to open your mind and heart. It will help you embrace the wealth of creativity that lives inside you. This is your human inheritance and your mirror of the divine.

MAGICAL CHILD

1. Picture a place where your Magical Child would most enjoy meeting with you. It might be a place where exploration and fantasy happen naturally, such as:
   Disneyland, Disney World or EPCOT Center
   Museum of Natural History or Art or Science
   Planetarium or Space Museum
   Movie studio tour

Concert hall or auditorium or theater
Dance studio or art studio
Mountain top
Island
Outer space
Under the sea.

2. Ask your Magical Child to draw a picture of itself through your non-dominant hand and to write its name on the picture.

3. Have a written conversation with your Magical Child. The adult voice writes with your dominant hand, the Magical Child speaks through your *other hand.* Get to know your Magical Child. Find out where it likes to go in the physical world as well as in imagination.

4. Find out who your Magical Child's favorite friends are. Who are its favorite
   artists
   actors/actresses
   musicians/composers/singers/performers
   writers/poets
   scientists/inventors/explorers
   heroes/heroines (fictional or historical).

5. Ask your Magical Child about its favorite books, stories, movies, plays, TV shows, records, performances, music.

6. Find out what your Magical Child's favorite activities are.

7. If your Magical Child could travel forward or backward in time, where would it want to go? Ask it to tell you all about it, maybe even draw a picture of such a time. What would it do on this trip?

8. Ask your Magical Child what role it has played in your life. How has it contributed to your development, your career, your hobbies, your achievements?

9. Ask your Magical Child to tell you one thing it would like to explore or create. Work out a mutually agreeable plan to take action on the Child's wish.
10. Thank your Magical Child for telling you about itself. If you are willing to meet again, tell the Child when and where.

Watch how your Magical Child comes out in day-to-day situations. Taking time out to feel and experience your Magical Child can give you a new perspective on life and unleash tremendous energy, vitality, and creativity. Embracing the world of the Magical Child has the power to bring happiness and greater fulfillment to all your endeavors.

Pamela is a wonderful example of someone who found a chest of riches when she discovered her Magical Child. In Chapter Six, she told how she healed her chronic sinus congestion by contacting a Vulnerable Child's "voice" within that wanted its mommy. Pamela poured out years of withheld tears and grief over the loss of her mother. Allowing that Child to express itself had a tangible, physical effect upon her health. This right/left-hand dialogue technique led the way to her Playful Child and then to her Magical Child. Here's Pamela's account of the fantastic changes she has experienced through integrating all parts of her Inner Child, Vulnerable as well as Playful and Magical, into her life:

> During my successful work with the Well-Being Journal Method, I started actively pursuing my true, secret love: creative writing. I was inspired to write a children's book and it came out in the form of a right/left-hand dialogue between a child of divorce and a Fairy Godmother figure named Roses. The child, who I called Amberanna, was really me. She was the sad and lonely child I had been when my parents divorced and left me with my grandparents. Roses was the personification of my Inner Self, who I had contacted through journal writing.

As I wrote, images kept popping into my head. Since I was not an "artist," I asked Lucia to recommend a professional who might be interested in illustrating this book. She protested and said firmly, "You, my dear, will illustrate the book yourself."

I was skeptical. Although I was interested in art, my artistic urges had long ago been crushed by my own critical voices. But a spark had been ignited and I set to work illustrating the book, which I have entitled, *Child's Song: A Beautiful Promise.*

Myname is
Amberanna. I want
to tell you about
adream I had. I
live with my
Grama and Grampa
in a house in the
woods. My mommy

Pamela also tells the story of how a right/left-hand dialogue helped her overcome another block: stage fright.

> After I'd worked with Lucia's methods for several years and had immersed myself in this art form and healing method, she invited me to be a guest on a TV show she was producing and hosting. I was going to talk about my healing experiences and the birth of my children's book. As excited and honored as I felt, I was also ready to refuse her invitation because of big, gnawing fears and feelings of inadequacy. My Little Child was terrified. Since I had used my journal dialogues as a tool for successfully coping with childish fears many times before, I put my pen in my left (non-dominant) hand and drew a picture of myself on television, looking baffled and afraid. Then I drew myself a second time, looking happy, and my left hand scrawled the words: "ON AND DOING FINE."
>
> This simple process somehow helped release my fears of appearing before the public and I did go on and I did fine.

LOVE TO
YOU,
DEAR CHILD

ON
AND DOING
FINE!!!

PAMELA'S PICTURE OF HERSELF WITH HER PLAYFUL AND MAGICAL CHILDREN.

Pamela, who once said she was no artist, went on to receive art training and now teaches children's art classes privately and in elementary schools.

Career changes like Pamela's are not unusual as a result of right/left-hand dialogues and drawings. Such major shifts happen all the time. When the Inner Child is included in career choices, creativity and enthusiasm are present. And deep down inside, we all know these are the true keys to success and fulfillment.

In my own career, the Playful Child and the Magical Child brought great joy to me and others. They were the parts of me who created a very special workshop called "Play Day for Grown-ups." We turned a large student faculty lounge at Los Angeles City College into a nursery school environment for these workshops. Grown-ups became kids for a day with finger paint, peanut butter and crackers, clay, crayons, costumes, toys, water guns, stuffed animals, baby bottles, and blankets. The results were incredible. Each time these workshops were held, people reported back to me that a profound inner healing had occurred. They experienced major changes in careers in the direction of their heart's desire as well as a general opening up of their creativity and expressiveness.

CHAPTER EIGHT

Reaching Out: Dialogues with Others

A man was walking along the road at night. He saw a piece of rope lying on the road. As soon as he saw that rope, he shouted, "Oh, this is a snake! This is a snake!" As soon as he recognized that rope as a serpent, his state of mind was upset and he got very scared. Then he completely lost his balance. When he was so scared, he even thought he saw the rope move a little bit, even though it actually was only a rope. Soon many people gathered to see where the serpent was. Someone said, "It is not a snake; it is a crack in the earth." Another said, "It is a water mark." In this way, everyone recognized that particular object according to his own understanding. By this time, nobody could come to the conclusion about what the object really was; everyone was giving his own idea. Then someone brought a lamp, and when they saw that object by lamplight they saw that it was only a rope. Then all delusions were removed. . . .

The Yoga Vasishtha *(an ancient Indian text) contains a great doctrine: the world is as you see it. . . . All the experiences that you undergo—whether you suffer loss or gain, pleasure or pain, happiness or sorrow; whether you are afflicted with negativities; or whether your heart is full of joy—are your own creations. Nobody else is responsible for them. Just as the world is as you see it, likewise, the state you are in depends on your attitude. One creates one's own destiny. We create our own heaven and our own hell, but we hold other things responsible for it, such as our country, or our government, or our destiny, or our parents, or the scheme of things. We become friends with one person and keep swaying in the joy of that friendship. We become hostile to another person and keep rejecting him all the time inside ourselves. But it is we who have created that friend and that enemy. Therefore, change your way of looking at things; make it divine. We meditate so that we may be able to see the world as it is.*

—Swami Muktananda

In the West, this philosophy—the world is as you see it—has been described in terms of mirrors and projections. Many psychologists are fond of saying, "It's all done with mirrors." By that they mean that relationships in the outer world are a mirror of the relationship we have with ourselves. We've all observed this in everyday life. When you're in a "good mood," it's easy to get along with others, to enjoy their company, to love them even when they are behaving unlovably. However, when you're in a bad mood, the same people with the same flaws in the same situations will set off an inner explosive. The outside world is the same, but *you* are different inside, so everything is changed.

So, "if it's all done with mirrors," if the external reality changes with your internal state, what are the implications? One solution has woven itself through numerous schools of thought, from ancient Eastern traditions to Western psychotherapies. That solution can be stated simply: "Change the inner picture and the outer picture will follow naturally."

How can we change our inner picture? How can we improve our lives by clearing up our own in-sight? One way is through drawings and inner dialogues done with the right and left hands. As you have seen from examples in previous chapters, this can be a powerful tool for knowing and changing one's life. You may have even had first-hand experiences of change from doing the exercises yourself.

Now, conversations with parts of the self are nothing new. In fact, dialogues provide the basis for many forms of psychotherapy, such as Gestalt Therapy, Transactional Analysis, Psychodrama, Voice Dialogue, and others. What is new is the convenient self-help aspect of written dialogues which access deeper levels of understanding from the right brain.

Dialogues which change your inner world directly affect the outer world, especially your relationships with others. When it comes to relationships, we are programmed to blame and change the other person. We want to change his mind, his beliefs, his actions, to accommodate our needs. We use the other as a scapegoat who then carries for us the characteristics we have judged and disowned. We indulge in what psychoanalysts call projection: superimposing our own mental picture on the screen of other individuals. We label ourselves right or good and call the other person wrong or bad. Does this sound familiar? Doesn't this echo the dichotomy between the right and left hand described in Chapter Two?

Another form of projection involves idol-worship or fantasy, in which we place qualities we value or need to develop onto another person, thinking that "they've got it" and we don't. We end up being dependent and feeling an emptiness in that part of ourselves. The more we try to get from the other person, the more pressure we exert. Projection always leads to disappointment. Idols topple from their pedestals; society's scapegoats retaliate through criminal behavior which affects us all.

One way to heal your relationships with others is to turn away from this outer struggle and engage in internal confrontation with yourself. In the case of conflict, there are two sides to every story and they can be written out by your right and left hands. When you do this, you take responsibility for the relationship with the other and put it into your own hands. Now there is a possibility of resolution, not by trying to change the other person, but by expanding your awareness.

I'd like to share with you a dramatic experience I had with the "mirror phenomenon." At the time I was training elementary school teachers to teach Creative Journal-keeping in the classroom. One of the teachers in my training group was resisting the new program with all her might. She chattered to her fellow teachers during in-service seminars to the point of being asked by the trainers to be quiet or leave the room. It was also becoming clear that she was bad-mouthing the program and trainers to her fellow teachers.

This went on for nearly a semester. By Christmas vacation, I was beside myself with frustration over this teacher's attitude and behavior. What should I do? I wasn't willing to put up with it any longer. That much I knew. Should I confront her openly? Should I go to the principal or project director and complain? Perhaps I could write an inner dialogue and, at the very least, get my feelings off my chest. I might even gain some insight. And that is what I did.

I started by telling her off in no uncertain terms. Using my left hand, in bold letters I called her names, told her what I thought of her, how I felt about her behavior.

I didn't even have to engage in written conversation, because as soon as I "told her off" with my left hand, a flash of insight lit up my mind. I saw her face before me and saw her *fear*! I could almost hear her saying, "I'm afraid of this new method. I'm afraid of failing and looking stupid. I don't want to change. That's why I'm fighting you." I was left with a feeling of compassion and empathy.

After Christmas vacation ended, I returned to school with some trepidation. I felt I understood why this teacher had been behaving so badly, but I still wondered what would happen.

I'll never forget my surprise that cold January morning as I walked up the path into the school. There she was, walking briskly toward me with a huge smile on her face. With great enthusiasm she invited me to visit her classroom, saying, "I'd like you to see the journal work my kids are doing. It's really wonderful. Would you come and visit during journal period this morning? They'll be sharing what they've written and drawn. Maybe you could talk to them about journals, too. They love their journals so much." She was a different person: open, calm, and confident. I was shocked and enormously pleased.

In Chapter Six, Jill shared a dialogue with her headache in which she embraced her Inner Child. Jill didn't stop with that first dialogue, though, for she knew there was more work to do. In private sessions with her counselor, she dialogued with her father.

Jill had felt like a victim most of her life. The roots of her feelings of victimization went back to her early years and her relationship with her father. He had raised the children alone, and Jill grew up feeling left out. She did a written dialogue with her father which focused on an incident in her youth that epitomized the unfair treatment she had received. She wrote her part with her dominant hand. Her father's response, which she wrote with her non-dominant hand, appears in italics.

Why didn't you give me anything when you brought my sister the compact?

I didn't want you to wear makeup. If you are a little girl, you are safe for me to deal with. When you were little I brought you toys, clay and balloons, but not grown-up things. When you were fifteen I started to give you money because I could not buy you anything anymore. I did not know you anymore. You had life and I was dead. I am afraid of life, can't you see that now? You would make me think about things I don't want to think about.

What sort of things?

I hated my life but I could not debate it. I was too weak. I did not dare want anything except what I was supposed to want. That's why I travel so much now, because I want my life to be different.

Didn't you know how much you were hurting me?

I didn't want to see you. I could not do anything to make you real to me.

Yet you resented me—you threw my things on the floor. You embarrassed me in front of your friends. You refused to see my needs. My sister was so obviously your favorite that even your own friends remarked on it.

I told myself you didn't need me. You seemed so ready to grasp life I was afraid of you. I wanted my peace and comfort and I didn't want you interfering with it. If you didn't wear makeup or bother me, I could pretend you didn't exist.

But I *do* exist and I am carrying around a lot of extra weight that I don't want. You always wanted to "cover me up," so I did it for you. I know we will never have a true, loving relationship. You are a poor, pathetic, lonely old man, who even now won't talk about *feelings*. I got gypped! This is not what a father should be. And yet I am somewhat sorry for you because you have alienated almost everyone who tried to care about you. I don't want you to have any more power over me.

> Aunt ______ told me she *begged* you to get a housekeeper for us and you wouldn't. You have never been able to see anyone else's need.
>
> *If I got a housekeeper I would have to admit I had no wife. I could not face that either, for then I would have had to admit my part in it.*
>
> What am I supposed to do now?
>
> *Rethink the past. Feel it the way it should have been . . . Make believe that you got a compact, too. You* should *have gotten one. Relive it in your mind with the proper ending. You are the only strong one of the four of us—the most beautiful and the wisest. You can still be what we could not. Please only yourself. Never mind what others say you should do. You will never hurt anyone if you live as you truly believe. Do it for me. I could not. Your mother could not. Your sister came closer but was satisfied with too little. The very thing I am afraid of is what will save you and carry you to great heights of love.*

In retrospect, Jill had this to say about her dialogue with her father:

> Writing privately in a journal, I could say things I couldn't say otherwise. I could also get him to say things I couldn't get out of him in any other way. But I knew they were so. I knew that was how he *really* felt.
>
> I stopped analyzing and alibiing for him and how unfairly he had treated me. I let my feelings out. When I did this, I realized that I had been helpless as a kid, but I am not helpless anymore. There are other alternatives. *That's the point!* People should know this.
>
> My biggest breakthrough was in burying the victim.

Through right/left handwriting, Jill gained insight into her father's fears, unhappiness, and feelings of inadequacy. After a lifetime of resentment, Jill released her anger at her father and finally accepted him for who he was instead of wishing he had been different. She could finally say "I love you" to him out loud, in person. "That's something we *never* did in our family," she said. "But I did it!"

Dialogues with others have proven to be great bridge-builders in times of conflict with or separation from another person. Many students have reported that such written conversations have opened doors to communication and intimacy with lovers, spouses, children, parents, siblings, and friends as well as employers, work associates, and other significant people in their lives.

There is no limit to the kinds of relationships that can be deepened or healed in this manner. You can dialogue with people living or dead, real or fictitious. Remember, if "it's all done with mirrors," it's all inside you anyway.

Do you have some unresolved feelings about a parent, mate, friend, work associate, or other individual? This next exercise, Two Sides to the Story, gives you a chance to express your unspoken feelings. It will also enable you to look at the other side of the conflict or estrangement *as it lives in you.* After both sides are out and understood, a deep healing of the split between you and the other person can take place.

TWO SIDES TO THE STORY

1. Using both hands, have a written dialogue with someone with whom you are in active conflict or from whom you are estranged. Write your voice with your dominant hand. Write the other person's voice with your non-dominant hand.

2. Tell the other person how you feel about him or her and about the relationship. Ask the other person how he/she feels about you.

3. Tell the other person how you want things to be between you and ask him/her to do the same.

> After this dialogue, watch what happens in your relationship with this other person. Notice whether your feelings and actions change. Is there any change in the other person's behavior?

Another way to own your part in a relationship is through letter writing. A letter from the *other hand* can be written for the writer but not necessarily sent. This is internal work. However, sometimes such a letter is so lucid that the writer decides to send it. If the writing is too illegible, it can be copied or typed before sending.

Erin dealt successfully with a problem relationship by writing a "private" letter with her *other hand.* She realized she couldn't change her friend, whose behavior toward Erin had become quite hostile. But she could take care of herself. The letter helped Erin clear her feelings and put closure on the relationship.

> Dear ______
>
> I am writing to you. I want to tell you that I forgive you for hurting me. I realize you're just trying to say I'm scared, I love you, please love me. I do love you and do forgive you. I'm happy that you love me. I want you to forgive me for all the ways that I have hurt you. I have been unwilling to let go of my own fear. I now am willing. I'm truly sorry. I now realize that we keep each other in our lives because we have many things to teach each other. We mirror to the other the tapes and movies that run in our heads.
>
> Our fight showed me how violently my inner critic & my inner child fight. Thank you for showing me that. I hope that you have found something of value out of our fight for you to learn. I believe that we all teach each other something about ourselves in our interaction.
>
> To continue our relationship I want only expressions of love. Fear isn't necessary. Affirmations of the other is the only way we will change and grow together. Please trust me that I will

choose the correct path for my life's goals. Whatever it may seem to you. I will trust that you too will choose the right paths for your life's purpose. I love you and I love myself.

Your best friend, Erin

As you can see, letter writing can be a vehicle for inner work on outer relationships. In the next exercise you'll be writing this kind of "private" letter meant for your eyes only. You'll be writing for yourself. The purpose is to get some feelings off your chest. The letter may be so clear that you may want to send it. That's fine if you do, but it's not the goal.

One of the great advantages of a private letter written for yourself is that you can tell—in straight talk—exactly how you feel without worrying about interruptions, reactions, or disapproval from the other person. It can help you get to the bottom of your emotions, so that when you do (if you do) communicate directly with the person, you can be clear and truthful. You may write a letter, talk on the phone or in person.

WRITE A LETTER

1. Think of a person to whom you'd like to express some feelings. They may be feelings of anger, resentment, or frustration, or they may be shyness, attraction, or love.
2. Write a spontaneous letter with your non-dominant hand. Tell this person how you feel about him or her, how you feel about the relationship, what you want and don't want.

If you decide to communicate all or part of your letter to the other person, you may want to type or rewrite it before you send it.

We have many kinds of relationships in our lives, with objects, projects, and environments as well as people, pets, and other living things. Anyone or anything can be "the other" in an inner conversation. Once, I was looking for a new residence and was having great difficulty finding the right place. I drew some sketches of the front of an "imaginary house" as well as a floor plan. Then I dialogued with the "future house" and learned a great deal about myself. The following is the dialogue I did with the "imaginary house" before I ever laid eyes on it. My *other hand* writing appears in italics.

I feel blocked about finding a house.

Don't blame that on me.

Are you the house or apt?

I'm the dwelling you want.

Why can't I have you now? Why are there so many seeming obstacles?

You haven't been ready.

But I'm so tired of feeling homeless.

Get clear on your inner home. That's where your heart is. When you locate that home you'll create the outer home. Do you understand?

Sort of. I just want a resting place. A place where I can lie down and truly rest.

That place is within. You are a weary traveler. It's true. I understand. In order to travel you need a home base inside. Understand how your outer environment is a symbol.

I feel so uprooted. Like my nerve endings/roots are hanging out and need earth and nourishment.

Let yourself have it.

Easier said than done.

Better done.

Why am I homeless?

So that you understand homelessness. Then you will appreciate me all the more when you find me.

A few weeks later, the house appeared. It was just as I had pictured it in my journal. This apparently "psychic" phenomenon was simply a demonstration of the power of the unconscious mind. My graphic picture was a magnet that drew to me the corresponding object which already existed in the three-dimensional world. My right-brain image enabled me to "recognize" the house while driving past on the way to another location. Upon seeing the "For Lease" sign, my rational mind's first reaction was critical. The affluent location didn't fit my concepts of what was affordable. But my visual right brain "remembered" the picture I had drawn, which resembled the house I was seeing with my eyes. It turned out that the house was affordable, and we moved in a week later.

The same technique of graphic visualization and dialogue can be applied to relationships that do not yet exist in physical reality. An example from one of my students will illustrate the principal of "manifesting from imagination."

Late one evening as I was dozing off to sleep, the phone on my night stand rang and jangled me abruptly out of the half-sleep state. I drowsily answered and heard a cheery voice apologizing for calling so late. It was Suzanne, a young woman who had attended my weekly journal workshop the previous year.

"I just had to call you," she explained. "You see, I'm getting married tomorrow and I HAD to thank you."

"Thank me?"

"Yes. You know that exercise you gave us where we drew and wrote out a description of a person we wanted to meet? And then we wrote a dialogue with the person. Well, I did the exercise. I described the mate I wanted. But then I forgot all about what I had written. Until a few months ago. I was dating this guy, Bill, and one night after we went out, I remembered that exercise I did in your class. So I found that journal and re-read that entry. It was amazing! I'd written a perfect description of Bill. I could hardly believe it. I hadn't even met him when I wrote that stuff. The next time we went out, he asked me to marry him and, of course, I said YES. And we're getting married tomorrow. And I'm so grateful to you."

"That's wonderful," I replied. "But if the marriage doesn't work out, I hope you won't blame it on me." We both had a good laugh and, as far as I know, they're still having a happy marriage.

In recent years, the issue of male-female relationships has come to the forefront as a major challenge. Certainly the "battle of the sexes" is nothing new. But it seems to be in the spotlight these days. The high divorce rate, the growing incidence of spouse abuse and sexual violence, and the current concern over AIDS and other sexually transmited diseases has forced us to pay attention to the nature of our relationships. Some have even called this the Post-Sexual Liberation Era.

Values are being seriously reconsidered and behaviors are being modified in the light of new physical risks and health hazards. Twelve-step programs have been created to deal with these issues, such as Sexoholics Anonymous and Sex and Love Addicts Anonymous. There is also a flood of self-help books on love and relationships. Some of these books have provided the basis for an entire movement of self-help groups, such as *Women Who Love Too Much*, which has spawned numerous groups and classes.

How can inner work help? What part can writing with the *other hand* play in sorting out the relationship mess that so many men and women find themselves in these days? Before sharing some techniques which have proven valuable in dealing with confusion and pain in "romantic" relationships and marriage, I'd like to quote one of my favorite Jungian analysts, author Linda Leonard. In her book, *On the Way to the Wedding*, Leonard gets right to the heart of the matter when she writes:

> The man or woman searching for a soul mate is seeking the divine, and often looks for the divine in a concrete person who has divinity within. But the human loved, like the lover,

is also finite and lives in the ordinary realm, thus ultimately disappointing when compared with the vision of divine love.

There is the ideal or pure love of romanticism on the one hand, which simply cannot be sustained on a day-to-day basis by ordinary mortals. On the other hand, there is a "practical" notion of love which easily becomes boring, materialistic, and lifeless. One family therapist describes these lifeless relationships by saying, "There's no juice there." We are back to dualism: heaven and earth, eternal and temporal, spirit and matter. How do we live with these opposites?

One way to honor the opposites is to honor them in ourselves. We do this by letting the opposites within us dialogue on paper. We also do this by asking ourselves what it is we want in a relationship, whether it's an ongoing marriage, partnership or any relationship we would like to have. The next exercise is intended to help you explore your values and desires regarding a love relationship. It will help you get clear on what you want and what you don't want. If you can see the qualities you are looking for in another person, you can own them in yourself as well. When you have done that, then you are open to attracting what you desire. Remember, like attracts like.

PORTRAIT OF A RELATIONSHIP

1. Using your non-dominant hand, draw a picture of the relationship you want. This does not have to be a realistic portrait of two people, although it can be. It may be a symbolic representation, a cartoon, or diagram. Whatever works for you. It is a portrait of the relationship you would like to have. Be sure to put yourself in the picture, too.
2. With your non-dominant hand, write a description of the person you would like to have a relationship with.
3. Write out a dialogue with the other person. You write with your dominant hand, the other person writes with your *other hand.*

See what happens in your daily life. Continue the dialogues with yourself to get crystal clear on what you want, how you want to feel and relate to the other person. And keep the following passage from Linda Leonard's *On the Way to the Wedding* in the back of your mind:

> The divine mating, the mystical marriage, is . . . an archetype at the very heart of our human existence. It is that vision which inspires the soul's sacred journey to the divine. And while we most often first project the divine wedding as a mystery to be found outside us, ultimately we come to find that the dance of the divine wedding is a wedding within.

CHAPTER NINE

The Hand of God Within

I saw my Lord with the eye of my heart,
and I said: Who art Thou? He said: Thou.

—Al-Hallaj

As fragrance abides in the flower
As the reflection is within the mirror
So does the Lord reside within Thee—
Why search for Him without?

—Nanak

Tat Tvam Asi
Thou art That
You are That—You are God.

—The Upanishads

DEEP IN THE RECESSES OF EVERYONE'S MIND
lives the knowledge
that God lives within the Self.
We try to deny this knowledge,
we try to ignore it,
we try to forget it.
Yet no matter how hard we try to hide it,
this knowledge, this truth emerges.
We do everything in our power
to avoid the truth.
We've separated ourselves from others,
from our real Selves,
from nature.
You need me to remind *you of the truth.*

—(Written by the other hand)

Truth is within you.
It is never any farther
away than your
beating heart.
You don't have to "think"
about it or go outside
searching for it.
You always contain it.

Somewhere along life's path, I "got the message" that God resides within the Self. This Self is not the ego, not the personality, but a greater power. I can't tell you exactly when the seed of this knowledge started to sprout. I only know that gradually, slowly, quietly, it took hold in the dark like an embryo. As it grew, its gestation was nourished and speeded up by the intense work I did during and after the life-threatening illness which led to right/left-hand dialoguing.

My search took me on extensive travels through the Southern California supermarket of personal growth offerings. I sampled many methods and read hundreds of books. And I kept coming back to the work of C. G. Jung. I had discovered Jung when I read *Man and His Symbols* during my illness in 1973. That book strongly influenced me to become an art therapist. As I contemplated that career change, I realized that the super-scientific mechanistic or behaviorist schools held no interest for me. For me, a psychology without a psyche (soul) was bankrupt. And Jung's work had "soul." As an artist, I responded to the rich visual imagery, the archetypes of myth and religion that Jung illuminated so beautifully.

Around the time I was deciding to get a degree in psychology, I saw a film about Jung which showed pages from his personal journal, *The Red Book*. I was stunned by the timeless quality of his paintings, by the ancient and universal symbolism I was so familiar with from my studies in art history. Most of all, I was struck by a painting of his inner guide, Philemon, a white-haired, bearded man with whom Jung conversed. Jung described him as follows:

> He said things which I had not consciously thought. For I observed clearly that it was he who spoke, not I.
>
> Psychologically, Philemon represented superior insight. At times he seemed to me quite real, as if he were a living personality. To me he was what the Indians call a guru.

Another scene that endeared Jung to me was one in which he was being interviewed. He is asked, "Dr. Jung, do you believe in God?" Old man Jung peers into the camera and responds with twinkling eyes, "I don't have to believe. I KNOW."

Jung's knowing about God extended to his clinical work as well. In the *Collected Works*, Jung wrote:

> Among all my patients in the second half of life—that is to say, over thirty-five—there has not been one whose problem in the last resort was not that of finding a religious outlook on

> life. None of them has been really healed who did not regain his religious outlook. This of course has nothing whatever to do with a particular creed or membership of a church.

Inspired by Jung's work, I took classes in metaphysics and began reading books on Eastern philosophies and spiritual practices. I consulted the ancient Chinese oracle, the *I Ching*, explored the images of the Tarot, and drew pictures of dreams and images from meditative states.

I kept getting the same message: "The answer lies within." During several years of self-therapy with the journal process, I tested the validity of that statement and found that it certainly was true for me. I had found so many answers within through drawing and writing that I started to ask, *Is this what God is? Is God this source of wisdom and consolation I tap into through wording and picturing?*

Then one day the God Within tapped me on the shoulder, so to speak. I was drawing with my dominant hand in my journal. A design emerged which resembled a top view of the human brain, showing the division between the two hemispheres. The connection between them was also shown in a continuous pair of figure eight loops with a sunburst at the center point.

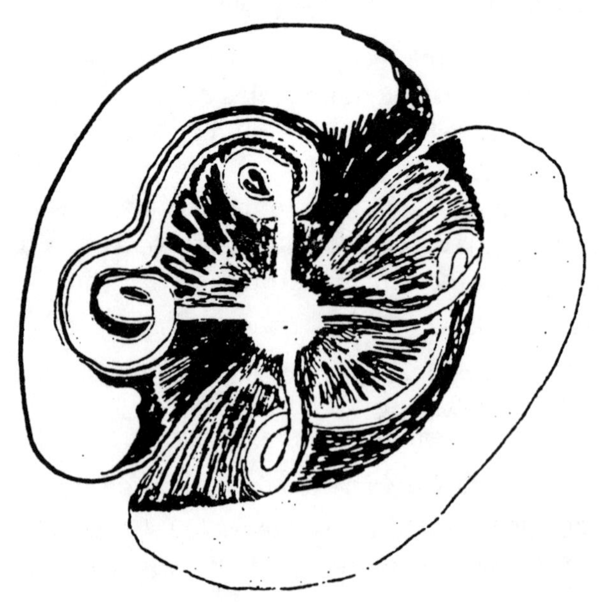

Then suddenly a poem appeared on the page, like the first green sprouting of spring. It wrote itself, much like automatic writing, with no conscious intent or editing on my part. It was written with my dominant (right) hand, yet the words flowed with the same spontaneity and simplicity I had come to associate with my left handwriting. This is the poem that happened:

> Hold me, echoes the whisper from within
> Hold me near you
> Hold me close to your heart
> as the apple of your eye
>
> Through the distant chambers of time
> our hearts beat
> as the wings of doves
> brush against the skies of eternity
>
> We were never parted
> for we are one through infinite
> space and time
>
> You have embraced me in shadow
> unbeknownst to my daytime self,
> always present behind me, above me, beneath
>
> You are the ground of my existence
> forever with and within me.

Sublime peace filled me as I completed the last line. I heard the "whisper from within" coming from my Inner Self. I acknowledged a divine power within and felt its presence. It was still "embracing me in shadow," yet I could say, "Yes, I know you are there." I remembered the film about Jung, the images of his inner guide, Philemon. Now I understood what Jung must have felt when he first contacted his inner wisdom voice in the form of that white-haired sage. Although I didn't see a form, I certainly felt its presence.

A couple of years later, I learned of a mantra. One of my students who was a devotee of the meditation master, Swami Muktananda, shared with me the mantra of Siddha Yoga: OM NAMAH SHIVAYA. It is Sanskrit for "I honor the God who dwells within my Self." The first time I encountered this mantra, I sobbed for a long time. I sobbed with all my heart. They were tears of joy, for I felt as if I had come home to my Self. After that, daily meditation became as much a part of my life as journal-keeping.

Shortly after the experience with the mantra, I had a dream that was so vivid it seemed to have actually happened in the waking state. Here is the dream:

> I am lying prostrate on the ground at the feet of a spiritual master. I cannot see a face or recognize who the master is, for I only see the feet and the hem of a robe. The feet are brown (like the skin of an East Indian) and the robe is crimson-red silk.
>
> I hear a voice from this master saying, "I want to live with you and within you."
>
> I say, "I surrender."

I awoke with a strong sense that a transformation had occurred in my dream, although I couldn't grasp it with my rational mind. I didn't know what I had surrendered to. My logical mind certainly wasn't ready for a guru. Yet the words echoed in my heart with great familiarity: "with you and within you." They were the words that had appeared in my poem a few years earlier.

It was around this time that a "voice" came through my *other hand* that was different from any I had known. It had an immediacy and power greater than my "daytime self" and was speaking directly to me. It began by commending me upon the workshop I had conducted that day:

> *You were a mirror, really giving my work in a way they could understand. I'm very pleased and I want to open many new doors for you. So be ready—prepare yourself for very high-level work—total dedication and joy in service. . . .*

> *Be a light unto yourself and to others. Shine like your crystal.* (I was wearing a large faceted crystal around my neck at the time.) *Transmit love all over the place. Help others, and for God's sake (for mine) and yours and others', BELIEVE IN MIRACLES. I want you as a channel for miracles. But you must stay clean and clear—the egotistical desires must be cleansed out of your system. Otherwise I can't work through you. Don't get lost in illusions. Always beware of that. You ("you") do nothing. Remember your little "ego" is simply a tool, a vehicle to be transformed. You can rise to the heights of service if you remember that. I can perform miracles of love through you if you'll let me. Let your beautiful feminine receptivity and passion and deep love shower my light upon the world. I am the lover you've been searching for. I'm the one you can surrender to completely and totally. I will guide you now.*
>
> I wept writing the last page. It felt like a male energy, like my Higher Self (would Jung call it my Animus?). I definitely felt like I had made contact with a lover . . . a male energy to whom I could surrender totally, with no reservations—a Christ energy—one that would never desert or betray me, never mislead or deceive me. (I'm teary just writing this.) One that would only give me truth, beauty, and goodness if I would but listen—
>
> *I will always be here.*
> *I have always been here.*
> *I am.*

From the tears that welled up in my eyes and the depth of feeling that flooded my heart, I knew I had contacted that "ground of my existence forever with and within me." The God Within had spoken directly through my *other hand.* There was no mistaking it. I experienced an inner marriage that is difficult to describe in words. In some respects, it fit the descriptions I'd read of mystical union with God. My whole being was filled with a feeling of inner peace, at-one-ment, and love. I knew that I was loved completely and unconditionally by a source of power residing deep within my very own Self. I truly felt the hand of God Within.

My next conversation with my God Self happened a few months later at a workshop I was co-leading. It began as a journal exercise, a letter to "Dear Self" in which my left hand responded:

I gave you everything you have. When you put yourself down you put me *down.*

Are you God?

I'm the God in you.

How can this be? Me talking to God? It seems too easy and natural. Like breathing. You're so human. Like George Burns in *Oh, God!*

Not far from the truth. I'm right here—in and around you. You were always waiting for God to descend from on high from some distant mountaintop. Or you'd have to go to the Himalayas or India or some place like that.

Well, yes. I hear what you are saying. But you know, I didn't rush off to see . . . those . . . gurus like some of my guru camp-follower friends were doing a few years ago—somehow, I knew God must be closer than that.

I'm closer than close.

Then what about all these gurus? Aren't they valuable?

Sure. I haven't got anything against gurus. Why, some of my best friends . . . you know.

You're downright silly. I didn't know God was silly.

Sometimes I'm silly. I'm always—I'm everything you are. I'm everything.

This is fun. You have a good sense of humor.

No wonder. I made you, didn't I? I'd have to have a sense of humor. You make me laugh.

This time I laughed out loud—huge belly-laughs. Boy, that God. What a character. You never knew what to expect.

I've continued having dialogues with the God Within. Sometimes in longhand, sometimes in printing. It may be the Laughing Buddha, the Holy Spirit, Dear Self. In one particularly humorous interchange, I was told:

> *I'm a manifestation of the Laughing Buddha. I'm the comedy of God . . . the laughing aspect, the play—It's all a huge joke anyway. Something to keep me amused. And you've "gotten it"—you see, you're laughing inside even now . . . Right?*
>
> Right. It's ridiculous.
>
> *Truth is very comical. God loves a good joke.*
>
> Yes, I remember the first time I wrote a Dear Self letter many years ago in my journal. It was really silly stuff. That was you, wasn't it?
>
> *Of course.*
>
> So you are my Self?
>
> *Yes, and I'm everyone's Self. Look, you know all this . . . Enlightenment is when you get the punch line and you laugh for the rest of your life.*
>
> This is so silly. I just want to giggle. I am giggling. It's crazy. Don't they put people away for giggling all the time?
>
> *Not if you play your cards right. You know the answer. Laughter is healing. So keep laughing and teach others to laugh. Not only will they not put you away, they'll pay you to laugh. They'll honor you with invitations and money and acknowledgement.*
>
> Can I really do that? I mean, isn't there something stilted about expecting to laugh or planning a situation where people will laugh?
>
> *Look, just stay in the light, be light, and you'll laugh and others will be infected by it and they'll get well. Laughter is the cure. Joy*

is the prescription, humor is the medication. Everything else is a waste of time. Laughter works faster than anything else.

Are the Selves the same?

Yes and know.

Oh, come on. Are you going to get punny and cryptic on me?

Yes . . . you are all different containers for the same essence. The champagne all comes out of the same vat . . . It's all the same . . . Laughter is God. That's why babies laugh a lot. They know who they are. When you "get it" you have to laugh—that's all you can do.

But isn't sorrow real or valuable?

Sorrow is a lesson to be learned on the way to bliss. Once you get to bliss, joy, ecstasy—you don't need sorrow anymore. I repeat—YOU DON'T NEED SORROW ANYMORE.

Amen!

What freedom! I feel so happy and complete within myself now. . . .

I continued teaching others to contact their Inner Wisdom, the God Self, through writing with the *other hand*. This form of inner dialogue proved to be as powerful for others as it had been for me.

A few months after that dialogue, I was visited by another profound dream.

> Swami Muktananda is sitting on a throne smiling at me. Suddenly, his image dissolves into a new image. It is myself—a blissful infant—as I appeared in photographs taken when I was six months old. But in the dream my baby-self is adult size. Muktananda seems to be saying, "Honor your Self. God exists in you as you."

Like my earlier "surrender" dream, this one had a living reality about it. That dream was a precious gift, for it gave me the *experience* of God Within. It also helped me understand how important it is to own our divine nature and not to project it out onto others. Muktananda seemed to be saying to me that the task of the guru, master, or teacher is to point me inward to the God dwelling within me. It was an important lesson and one that was to surface for society as a whole: the Jim Jones massacre, the minister and guru scandals, the "psychic" scams. These events all seemed to be underscoring the need to find God Within instead of projecting God onto an image in the external world.

Later, I also came to understand how essential it is to develop a personal relationship with the divine Inner Self. I encounter many people seeking "quick fixes" from intermediaries channeling information from disembodied spirits. For me, the only message worth channelling is the truth of the Inner Self, the God that Dwells Within. To channel messages from disembodied entities with doubtful credentials seems like the little leagues compared to the pure gold of the Inner Self.

The next exercise is intended to help you communicate directly with your own voice of wisdom, your Inner Self or Greater Power. Whatever name you wish to call it is fine. And if you feel it is unnameable, that's fine, too.

DEAR INNER SELF

1. Focus on your experience of God or the Greater Power as you know it. Feel its presence or its energy. It may appear as a Christ energy or the presence of a particular spiritual teacher or leader, such as Buddha. Tune in to the image or presence that you experience as a guide to your own divinity.

2. Write a dialogue with this divine presence. Give it a name if you wish. Let the divine presence write with your non-dominant hand. With your dominant hand, ask questions or say anything you wish to express to this presence.

After beginning work on this book, doing research, and writing for many months, I was forced to put it on the shelf and attend to other things, practical things like making a living and dealing with personal life changes. After a few years I returned eagerly to the manuscript with the intention of completing the book. I had recently begun the practice of daily meditation upon the Inner Self. When I got to this chapter, I asked the Inner Self to tell me what to say. Naturally, I turned to my *other hand.* And so I will let the *other hand* have the last word.

So I asked "it," my Inner Self, to tell me what to say. Naturally, I turned to my other hand.

Just say that the deepest well of inner knowing and of peace is within everyone. It can be reached, in stillness, in quiet, and in solitude.

I am here in everyone and everything and the glory of being human is that you can know and ex-

perience at-one-ment with
me. For we are one.
When you are afraid,
lost, doubting — be
still, go inside and
find your True Self.
I will be there - where
I've always been -
waiting for you to
recognize the truth
of who you really
are

I will speak through everything that is so human in you – your feelings, your wishes, your body, your relationships.

How do I know I'm not just making you up out of my imagination? How do I know that you really exist?

You will know. If you don't recognize me at first, eventually you will. Sometimes when you have lost your

way and are far away
from your true Self,
you may doubt that I
exist. That is when you
have forgotten who _you_
really are. But if you
will speak with me,
as you are now, I will
respond. Later on
when you read our
conversation, you will
recognize my real-
ness. You will see
your own doubting

mind, and you will
feel my essence
and know it to be
yours. You will see
the difference between
your small, fearful,
anxious self and your
true, beautiful and
peaceful Self. And
since you have
written both voices,
you'll realize

that they both came from you. Then you will see that the Highest Truth and Wisdom resides within you. Everything else is illusion. You will see that you've had it backwards all these years. You thought your

self was the little, scared, confused "character" that doubts and worries and defends itself. That is the figment of imagination. That is the thing you made up with your mind.
I am the Real You. I am your True Self reminding you to wake up, come home

to the bliss of your
Inner Self.

Bibliography

Barsley, Michael. *Some of My Best Friends Are Left-Handed People: An Investigation into the History of Left-Handedness.* North Hollywood, CA: Wilshire Book Co., 1968.

Bentov, Itzhak. *Stalking the Wild Pendulum: On the Mechanics of Consciousness.* New York: Dutton, 1977.

Blakeslee, Thomas R. *The Right Brain: A New Understanding of the Unconscious Mind and Its Creative Powers.* Garden City, NY: Anchor Press/Doubleday, 1980.

Bliss, James, and Joseph Morella. *The Left-Hander's Handbook.* New York: A & W Visual Library, 1980.

Borysenko, Joan. *Minding the Body, Mending the Mind.* Reading, MA: Addison-Wesley, 1987.

Brown, Mark. *Left-Handed: Right-Handed.* North Pomfret, VT: David and Charles, Inc., 1979.

Capacchione, Lucia. *The Creative Journal: The Art of Finding Yourself.* Athens, OH: Ohio University/Swallow Press, 1979.

———. *The Well-Being Journal: The Art of Self-Care.* Santa Monica, CA: Lucia Capacchione, 1984.

———, and Elizabeth Johnson. *The Lighten Up Journal: Making Friends With Your Body.* Santa Monica, CA: Lucia Capacchione, 1986.

Capra, Fritjof. *The Turning Point: Science, Society, and the Rising Culture.* New York: Bantam Books, 1983.

Clarke, Molly Deane. *Healing the Inner Child.* A Guidebook and Four Tapes. Lummi Island, WA: Molly Deane Clark, 1987.

Cousins, Norman. *Anatomy of an Illness as Perceived by the Patient.* New York: Bantam Books, 1981.

Domhoff, G. Williams. "But Why Did They Sit on the King's Right in the First Place?" in *The Psychology of Human Consciousness.* Robert Ornstein, ed. San Francisco, CA: W. H. Freeman, 1968.

Dychtwald, Ken. *Body Mind.* Los Angeles: J. P. Tarcher, 1977.

Edwards, Betty. *Drawing on the Right Side of the Brain: A Course in Enhancing Creativity and Artistic Confidence.* Los Angeles: J. P. Tarcher, 1979.

Fincher, Jack. *Lefties: The Origins and Consequences of Being Left-Handed.* New York: Perigree Books, 1980.

Fritz, Nell. *Journey Into Me: The Twelve Step Workbook for Everyday Problems.* Irvine, CA: Journey Company, 1984.

Gazzaniga, Michael, and Joseph E. Le Doux. *The Integrated Mind.* New York: Plenum Press, 1978.

Gilling, Dick, and Robin Brightwell. *The Human Brain.* London: Orbis, 1982.

Hampden-Turner, Charles. *Maps of the Mind: Charts and Concepts of the Mind and Its Labyrinths.* New York: Collier Books, 1982.

Harman, Willis, and Howard Rheingold. *Higher Creativity: Liberating the Unconscious for Breakthrough Insights.* Los Angles: J. P. Tarcher, 1984.

Jaffe, Aniela, ed. *C. G. Jung: Word and Image.* Princeton, NJ: Princeton University Press, 1983.

Jaynes, Julian. *The Origins of Consciousness in the Breakdown of the Bicameral Mind.* Boston: Houghton Mifflin, 1976.

Joy, W. Brugh. *Joy's Way: A Map for the Transformational Journey.* Los Angeles: J. P. Tarcher, 1979.

Jung, Carl Gustav. *The Collected Works of C. G. Jung.* Princeton, NJ: Princeton University Press, 1970.

———. *Memories, Dreams, Reflections.* New York: Pantheon Books, 1963.

———, and M. L. von Franz. *Man and His Symbols.* Garden City, NY: Doubleday, 1964.

Leonard, Linda Schierse. *On the Way to the Wedding: Transforming the Love Relationship.* Boston: Shambala, 1986.

Miller, Alice. *For Your Own Good: Hidden Cruelty in Child-Rearing and the Roots of Violence.* New York: Farrar, Straus & Giroux, 1983.

Missildine, W. Hugh. *Your Inner Child of the Past.* New York: Pocket Books, 1982.

Muktananda, Swami. *Understanding Siddha Yoga.* Ganeshpuri, India: Gurudev Siddha Peeth, 1978.

Needham, Rodney, ed. *Right and Left: Essays on Dual Symbolic Classification.* Chicago: University of Chicago Press, 1973.

Ornstein, Robert. *The Psychology of Consciousness.* San Francisco: W. H. Freeman, 1972.

———, ed. *The Nature of Human Consciousness.* San Francisco: W. H. Freeman, 1973.

———, and David Sobel. *The Healing Brain: Breakthrough Discoveries About How the Brain Keeps Us Healthy.* New York: Simon & Schuster, 1987.

Oyle, Irving. *The Healing Mind.* Berkeley, CA: Celestial Arts, 1979.

Pearce, Joseph Chilton. "Breakthrough into Insight." *Darshan* 4 (May 1987). South Fallsburg, NY: SYDA Foundation.

Pelletier, Kenneth R. *Mind as Healer, Mind as Slayer: A Holistic Approach to Preventing Stress Disorders.* New York: Delta, 1977.

———. *Toward a Science of Consciousness.* New York: Delta, 1979.

Pollard, John K. *Self Parenting: The Complete Guide to Your Inner Conversations.* Malibu, CA: Generic Human Studies Publishing, 1987.

Restak, Richard M. *The Brain: The Last Frontier.* New York: Warner Books, 1980.

Rico, Gabriele. *Writing the Natural Way: Using Right-Brain Techniques to Release Your Expressive Powers.* Los Angeles: J. P. Tarcher, 1983.

Rilke, Rainer Maria. *Letters to a Young Poet.* New York: Norton, 1954.

Russell, Peter. *The Brain Book.* New York: Hawthorn Books, 1979.

Samples, Bob. *The Metaphoric Mind: A Celebration of Creative Consciousness.* Reading, MA: Addison-Wesley, 1981.

Schaef, Anne W. *Co-Dependence: Misunderstood-Mistreated.* New York: Harper & Row, 1986.

Segalowitz, Sid. *Two Sides of the Brain: Brain Lateralization Explored.* Englewood Cliffs, NJ: Prentice Hall, 1983.

Siegel, Bernie. *Love, Medicine & Miracles: Lessons Learned About Self-Healing from a Surgeon's Experience with Exceptional Patients.* New York: Harper & Row, 1986.

Springer, Sally, and Georg Deutsch. *Left Brain, Right Brain.* San Francisco: W. H. Freeman, 1981.

Stone, Hal, and Sidra Winkelman. *Embracing Our Selves.* Marina del Rey, CA: DeVorss & Co., 1985.

Whitfield, Charles L. *Healing the Child Within.* Pompano Beach, FL: Health Communications, 1987.

Wilber, Ken, ed. *The Holographic Paradigm and Other Paradoxes.* Boulder, CO: Shambala, 1982.

Wile, Ira S. *Handedness: Right and Left.* Boston: Lothrop, Lee & Shepard, 1934.

Zdenek, Marilee. *The Right-Brain Experience: An Intimate Program to Free the Powers of Your Imagination.* New York: McGraw-Hill, 1983.

J. C.
P.O Box 5805
San Monica CA. 90405